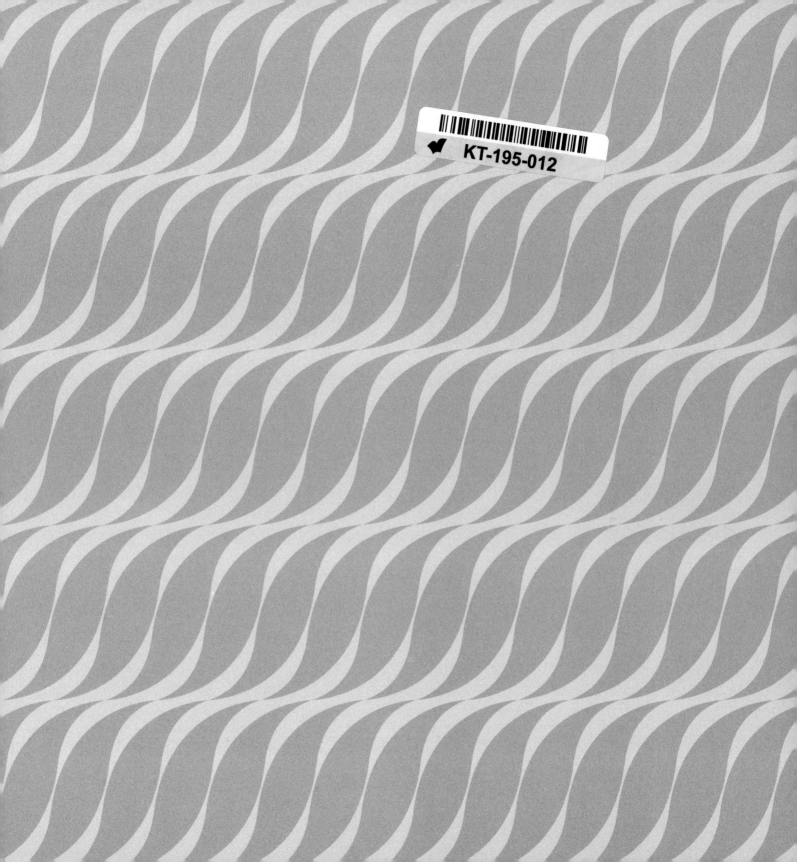

KT-195-012

LOW FAT
Pasta

LOW FAT
Pasta

SUE MAGGS

Photography by Peter Reilly

southwater

This edition is published by Southwater

Southwater is an imprint of Anness Publishing Ltd
Hermes House, 88–89 Blackfriars Road, London SE1 8HA
tel. 020 7401 2077; fax 020 7633 9499
www.southwaterbooks.com; info@anness.com

UK agent: The Manning Partnership Ltd, 6 The Old Dairy,
Melcombe Road, Bath BA2 3LR; tel. 01225 478444; fax 01225 478440;
sales@manning-partnership.co.uk

UK distributor: Grantham Book Services Ltd, Isaac Newton Way,
Alma Park Industrial Estate, Grantham, Lincs NG31 9SD;
tel. 01476 541080; fax 01476 541061; orders@gbs.tbs-ltd.co.uk

North American agent/distributor: National Book Network,
4501 Forbes Boulevard, Suite 200, Lanham, MD 20706;
tel. 301 459 3366; fax 301 429 5746; www.nbnbooks.com

Australian agent/distributor: Pan Macmillan Australia, Level 18,
St Martins Tower, 31 Market St, Sydney, NSW 2000; tel. 1300 135 113;
fax 1300 135 103; customer.service@macmillan.com.au

New Zealand agent/distributor: David Bateman Ltd,
30 Tarndale Grove, Off Bush Road, Albany, Auckland;
tel. (09) 415 7664; fax (09) 415 8892

Publisher: Joanna Lorenz
Senior Cookery Editor: Linda Fraser
Designer: Alan Marshall
Photographer: Peter Riley
Stylist: Jo Harris

Previously published as *Step-by-step Low Fat Pasta*

For all recipes, quantities are given in both metric and imperial
measures, and, where appropriate, measures are also given in
standard cups and spoons. Follow one set, but not a mixture,
because they are not interchangeable.

1 3 5 7 9 10 8 6 4 2

CONTENTS

INTRODUCTION

Pasta contains very little fat and is therefore an ideal food on
which to base a low-fat diet.

Pasta is high in filling "complex" carbohydrate, and when broken down by the
body, it allows a steady release of energy to keep us satisfied for a longer
period of time. It is also very versatile and accommodates a wide range of
additional flavours. A nutritious and satisfying meal can be made simply by
combining any pasta with a low-fat sauce or dressing.

Nutritionists recommend that half our daily diet is made up of "complex"
carbohydrates, which also include bread, potatoes, cereal, rice and most fruits.
They also recommend a reduction in fat intake, especially saturated fat, to
lessen the risk of heart disease.

Pasta comes in a wide variety of shapes, colours and flavours to suit all tastes.
This book recommends certain types of pasta, but don't worry if you can't find
the exact variety suggested – just use any similar pasta shape.

A general rule is that long strands such as spaghetti and tagliatelle work best
with thinner sauces, while short pasta shapes are good with chunky, meaty
sauces. Sheets of pasta are ideal for layered, baked dishes, and
tiny shapes are added to soups.

Whatever you choose, this book will show you how to keep the fat content of
the dishes low, so that you and your family can enjoy your meals and look
after your health at the same time.

Dried Pasta

This is a good standby as it can be kept for months in an airtight container. Look for the words "durum wheat" on the packet, as this is top quality pasta which produces good results. Always follow the manufacturer's instructions when cooking dried pasta, and when working out portions, remember that pasta can increase in volume as much as four times when cooked.

Anellini
Small pasta rings, sometimes serrated. They are good in soups and casseroles (1).

Campanelle
Twisted with frilled edges (2).

Cannelloni
Pasta tubes traditionally stuffed with a meat or cheese filling and baked in the oven (3).

Conchiglie
Pasta shells – they are smooth or ridged (rigate). The smaller shells are called conchigliette. The largest shells (conchiglioni) can be stuffed (4).

Elicoidali (rigatoni)
Good served with chunky sauces, or in baked dishes (5).

Farfalle (pasta bows)
Pasta in bow shapes, usually with decorated edges. They are ideal for "dressing up" a plain-looking salad (6).

Fettuccine
Long, narrow ribbons of pasta made from egg pasta. It is not as wide as tagliatelle (7).

Fusillata casareccia
These twists of pasta are good with tomato sauce (8).

Fusilli
Corkscrew-shaped pasta that works well with tomato and vegetable sauces (9).

Lasagne
Wide sheets of pasta, often layered between meat and vegetable sauces and baked. Usually the lasagne has to be cooked before baking, but pre-cooked varieties are available. Dried lasagne has smooth or wavy-edged sheets (10).

Macaroni
Hollow tubes of pasta – they are often served in baked dishes with a cheese sauce (11).

Mafaldine
Long wavy-edged strips of pasta (lasagnette) often eaten with soft cheeses such as Ricotta (12).

Pappardelle
Wide ribbons of egg pasta occasionally with wavy edges. They are a good accompaniment to meat or creamy sauces (13).

Penne
Quills of pasta in different sizes often with diagonal cuts for catching more sauce. They are available in both smooth and ridged varieties (14).

Pipe
Tubular pasta that comes either ridged (rigate) or plain (15).

Spaghetti
Long, very thin sticks of pasta – a traditional favourite in tomato or oily sauces (16).

Spirali
Short pasta spirals – they are versatile enough to be used in sauces or soups (17).

Stelline
These little pasta stars are often used in soups (18).

Tagliatelle
Long, flat strands of pasta that go well with creamy sauces. Tagliatelle verdi is green because it has had chopped spinach added to the dough. Squid-ink tagliatelle is manufactured by colouring pasta dough with the ink from squid (19).

Equipment

If you are using dried or shop-bought fresh pasta you will only need basic cooking equipment, but if you are making pasta dough there are a few time-saving gadgets that are fun to use and will help you to make pasta to be proud of!

Bowls
A set of bowls in different sizes is useful for mixing and whisking pasta sauce ingredients or for making pasta dough.

Chopping board
Nylon boards are easy to clean and more hygienic for chopping and cutting.

Colander
Essential for quickly draining cooked pasta and vegetables for pasta sauces.

Cook's knife
A large cook's knife with a sharp pointed blade is essential for cutting and chopping vegetables and meat for sauces.

Flour dredger
For lightly dusting sheets of pasta or work surfaces to prevent dough from sticking.

Measuring spoons
Vital for measuring small quantities accurately.

Non-stick saucepan
Used for browning meat without additional fat, and for sweating vegetables in stock as a basis for sauces and stews.

Pasta machine or roller
A small hand-operated machine (as shown opposite) is easy to use – it will knead, roll and cut pasta. Various attachments exist for different pasta shapes. Electric pasta machines are also available, but are probably only worth the money if pasta-making is a regular hobby.

Pasta or pastry wheel
Gives an impressive looking decorative edge if you are making ravioli or farfalle.

Pastry brush
For brushing fresh pasta with water, milk or beaten egg before sealing in the filling.

Pestle and mortar
For hand-grinding ingredients to a paste or powder. It is very useful for grinding pasta sauce essentials such as garlic, fresh herbs and spices.

Ravioli cutter
Round or square cutters for stamping out individual ravioli. Pastry cutters will also give very good results.

Ravioli tray (raviolatore)
A metal tray with hollows to make even-size ravioli. Usually sold with a small rolling pin which is used to seal and cut the ravioli on the serrated edges.

Rolling pin
For rolling out fresh pasta dough into thin sheets. Special pasta pins can also be bought – they are long, thin pieces of wood, but an ordinary rolling pin is easier to use.

Small grater
For grating whole nutmeg and Parmesan cheese.

Vegetable knife
At least one small knife like this is essential for preparing all kinds of vegetables.

Whisk
Useful for beating eggs and combining sauces.

Wooden spoon
For stirring and thickening pasta sauces and for gently easing pasta strands into boiling water as they soften.

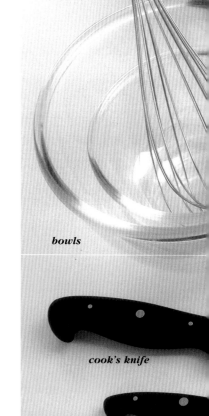

non-stick saucepan

whisk

bowls

cook's knife

pasta machine

colander

flour dredger

ravioli cutter

ravioli tray

rolling pin

pastry brush

pestle and mortar

measuring spoons

pastry wheel

vegetable peeler

wooden spoon

small grater

chopping board

vegetable knife

Do we need fat in our diet?

We only need 10 g/¼ oz fat in our daily diet for our bodies to function properly. A totally fat-free diet would be almost impossible to achieve, since some fat is present in virtually every food.

A certain amount of essential fatty acids are necessary in our diet to help our bodies absorb vitamins A, D, E and K as they are fat-soluble and cannot be made by the body. Fat is also needed to make hormones. Recent research has proved that we all eat far too much fat. Doctors now recommend that we limit our fat intake to no more than 30% of our total daily calorie intake, even as low as 25% for a really healthy diet. Some fats in the diet are a contributory factor in heart disease and cancers, such as breast, prostate and colon.

Types of fat in foods
Saturated fats are hard fats found in meat, most dairy products, such as butter, cream, dripping, hard margarines, cheeses and animal fats. Palm and coconut oil are also high in saturated fats. Saturated fats can raise the blood cholesterol level and clog up the arteries. The way we prepare and cook foods can limit the amount of saturated fat that we consume.

Polyunsaturated fats are soft fats such as sunflower, safflower, grapeseed, soya and corn oils, and fish such as mackerel, salmon or herring and nuts, seeds, cereals, lean meats and green vegetables. These fats may help to reduce our cholesterol levels.

Mono-unsaturated fats should make up most of the fat in our diet. They appear to have a protective effect and help lower cholesterol levels. Olive oil, rapeseed oil, peanut oil and avocados are all rich sources of mono-unsaturated fats.

A selection of foods containing the three main types of fat found in foods.

Eating a healthy low-fat diet

Eat a good variety of different foods every day to make sure you get all the nutrients you need.

1 Skimmed milk contains the same amount of calcium, protein and B vitamins as whole milk, but a fraction of the fat.
2 Natural low-fat yogurt, cottage cheese and fromage frais are all high in calcium and protein, and are good substitutes for cream.
3 Starchy foods such as rice, bread, potatoes, cereals and pasta should be eaten at every meal. These foods provide energy and some vitamins, minerals and dietary fibre.
4 Vegetables, salads and fruits should form a major part of the diet, and about 450 g/1 lb should be eaten each day.
5 Eat meat in moderation but eat plenty of fish, particularly oily fish such as mackerel, salmon, tuna, herring and sardines.

A few simple changes to a normal diet can reduce fat intake considerably. The following tips are designed to make the change to a healthier diet as easy as possible.

Meat and poultry
Red meats such as lamb, pork and beef are high in saturated fats, but chicken and turkey contain far less fat. Remove the skin before cooking and trim off any visible fat. Avoid sausages, burgers, patés, bacon and minced beef. Buy lean cuts of meat and skim any fat from the surface of stocks and stews.

Dairy products
Replace whole milk with skimmed or semi-skimmed and use low-fat yogurt, low-fat crème fraîche or fromage frais instead of cream. Eat cream, cream cheese and hard cheeses in moderation. There are reduced-fat cheeses on the market with 14% fat content which is half the fat content of full fat cheese. Use these wherever possible.

Spreads, oils and dressings
Use butter, margarine and low-fat spreads sparingly. Try to avoid using fat and oil for cooking. If you have to use oil, choose olive, corn, sunflower, soya, rapeseed and peanut oils, which are low in saturates. Look out for oil-free dressings and reduced fat mayonnaise.

Hidden fats
Biscuits, cakes, pastries, snacks and processed meals and curries all contain high proportions of fat. Get into the habit of reading food labels carefully and looking for a low-fat option.

Cooking methods
Grill, poach and steam foods whenever possible. If you do fry foods, use as little fat as possible and pat off the excess after browning, with kitchen paper. Make sauces and stews by first cooking the onions and garlic in a small quantity of stock, rather than frying in oil.

A selection of foods for a healthy low-fat diet.

Fresh pasta

Sheets of lasagne, and long ribbon-like pasta – tagliarini, fettuccine and tagliatelle are most commonly found in the fresh pasta section of supermarkets or delicatessens. Manufacturers are constantly adding to their ranges and although there are many varieties of dried pasta, a wide choice of fresh pasta is now available.

Fresh pasta is not necessarily better than dried, but buying it fresh offers the opportunity to choose a ready-stuffed variety. Popular ready-filled types are ravioli, agnolotti ("little slippers"), tortellini, tortelloni and cappelletti ("little peaked hats"). Fillings include spinach and ricotta, minced beef and ham. Pasta is often made from flavoured dough to complement the filling. If the filling looks quite rich, the calorie count can be kept down by combining the pasta with an uncomplicated sauce. Easier still, simply toss it in a little olive oil or low-fat margarine and sprinkle over some fresh chopped herbs.

Cooking fresh pasta usually takes much less time than for dried pasta, as fresh pasta still contains moisture. As with dried pasta, it is best to follow the cooking instructions given on the packet since the ingredients may vary.

For the best fresh pasta of all, nothing beats making it yourself. Once you have mastered the technique for basic pasta dough, you can add delicious fresh ingredients like finely chopped spinach, tomato purée and herbs to the dough to give extra colour and flavour.

Fresh pasta should always be stored in the fridge or freezer until ready for cooking. Make sure that you check the storage time on the packet.

tagliarini

cappelletti

cheese and tomato agnolotti

mini ravioli

gemelli

fusilli

tortellini

tortellini

tagliatelle

egg mafaldine

ravioli (small and large tomato)

Flavourings for low-fat sauces

Some ingredients seem to be made for pasta dishes. Take onions, garlic and tomatoes – three ordinary, everyday ingredients that blend easily with pasta and other ingredients to produce some extraordinarily good low-fat dishes.

To compensate for the lack of fat in the form of butter, oil, cream and full-fat cheeses, the recipes in this book make good use of the rich flavours of onions, garlic, concentrated sauces, fresh herbs and spices.

Skimmed milk and reduced-fat cheeses have been used wherever possible in the recipes. Remember that hard cheeses, such as Parmesan or Cheddar, are very high in fat. The wonderful strong flavour of Parmesan cheese can, however, still be enjoyed if used sparingly or handed out in a separate dish to be sprinkled or shaved on top of individual pasta portions.

Low-fat cheeses or yogurt have a fraction of the fat content of their full-fat equivalents.

Robust ingredients such as fresh chillies, fresh root ringer, lemon, or wholegrain mustard can all be used to help flavour the sauces.

Dried mushrooms and sun-dried tomatoes (not the varieties preserved in olive oil) are full of concentrated flavour and add an exotic richness to a pasta sauce.

The aromatic flavours of fresh herbs such as bay leaves, parsley, basil, coriander, oregano, rosemary and thyme add fragrance and colour to pasta sauces.

thyme

red onions

purple basil

ginger

Parmesan cheese

garlic

tomatoes

dried mushrooms (porcini)

flat leaf
parsley

rosemary

bay leaves

wholegrain
mustard

coriander
seeds

anchovy
fillets

green chilli

paprika

red chillies

carbonara sauce

tomato
pickle

pesto
sauce

lemon

tomato
purée

sun-dried
tomatoes

turmeric

fennel
seeds

TECHNIQUES

Basic Pasta Dough

Serves 3–4

INGREDIENTS
200 g/7 oz/1³/₄ cups plain flour
pinch of salt
2 eggs
10 ml/2 tsp cold water

Making pasta on a work surface

1 Sift the flour and salt on to a clean work surface and make a well in the centre with your hand.

2 Put the eggs and water into the well. Using a fork, beat the eggs gently together, then gradually draw in the flour from the sides, to make a thick paste.

3 When the mixture becomes too stiff to use a fork, use your hands to mix to a firm dough. Knead the dough for about 5 minutes, until smooth. (This can be done in an electric food mixer fitted with a dough hook). Wrap in clear film to prevent it drying out and leave to rest for 20–30 minutes.

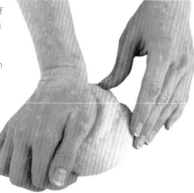

Making pasta in a bowl

1 Sift the flour and salt into a glass bowl and make a well in the centre. Add the eggs and water.

3 When the mixture becomes too stiff to use a fork, use your hands to mix to a firm dough. Knead the dough for 5 minutes until smooth. (This can be done in an electric food mixer fitted with a dough hook). Wrap in clear film to prevent it drying out and leave to rest for 20–30 minutes.

2 Using a fork, beat the eggs gently together, then gradually draw in the flour from the sides, to make a thick paste.

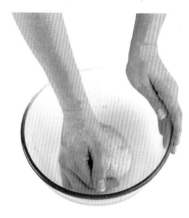

VARIATIONS
TOMATO: add 20 ml/4 tsp concentrated tomato purée to the eggs before mixing.
SPINACH: add 115 g/4 oz frozen spinach, thawed and squeezed of excess moisture. Liquidize with the eggs, before adding to the flour.
HERB: add 45 ml/3 tbsp finely chopped fresh herbs to the eggs before mixing the dough.
WHOLEMEAL: use 150 g/5 oz wholemeal flour and 50 g/2 oz plain flour. Add an extra 10 ml/2 tsp cold water (wholemeal flour will absorb more liquid than plain flour).
PAPRIKA: use 5 ml/1 tsp ground paprika sifted with the flour.

Rolling out pasta dough by hand

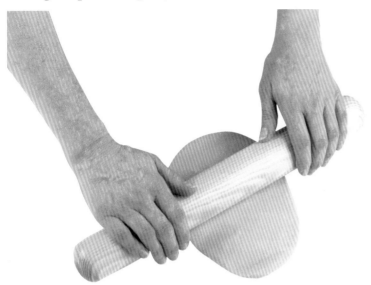

1 Cut the basic dough in quarters. Use one quarter at a time and re-wrap the rest in clear film, so it does not dry out. Flatten the dough and dust liberally with flour. Start rolling out the dough, making sure you roll it evenly.

2 As the dough becomes thinner, keep on rotating it on the work surface by gently lifting the edges with your fingers and supporting it over the rolling pin. Make sure you don't tear the dough.

3 Carry on rolling out the dough until it has reached the desired thickness, about 3 mm/⅛ in thick.

Rolling out dough using a pasta machine

1 Cut the basic dough into quarters. Use one quarter at a time and re-wrap the rest in clear film, so it does not dry out. Flatten the dough and dust liberally with flour. Start with the machine set to roll at the thickest setting. Pass the dough through the rollers several times, dusting the dough from time to time with flour until it is smooth.

2 Fold the strip of dough into three, press the joins well together and pass through the machine again. Repeat the folding and rolling several times on each setting.

3 Guide the dough through the machine but do not pull or stretch it or the dough will tear. As the dough is worked through all the settings, it will become thinner and longer. Guide the dough over the back of your hand, as the dough is rolled out to a thin sheet. Pasta used for stuffing, such as ravioli or tortellini, should be used straight away. Otherwise lay the rolled sheets on a clean dish towel, lightly dusted with sifted flour, and leave to dry for 10 minutes before cutting. This makes it easier to cut and prevents the strands of pasta sticking together.

Cutting pasta shapes

Until you are confident at handling and shaping pasta dough, it is easier to work with small quantities. Always keep the dough well wrapped in clear film to prevent it drying out, until you are ready to work with it.

Shaping ravioli

Cutting out spaghetti
To cut spaghetti, fit the appropriate attachment to the machine or move the handle to the appropriate slot. Cut the pasta sheets into 25 cm/10 in lengths and pass these through the machine. Guide the strands over the back of your hand as they appear out of the machine.

Cutting out tagliatelle
To cut tagliatelle, fit the appropriate attachment to the machine or move the handle to the appropriate slot. Cut the pasta sheets into 25 cm/10 in lengths and pass these through the machine as for spaghetti.

1 To make square ravioli, place spoonfuls of filling on a sheet of dough at intervals of 5–7.5 cm/2–3 in, leaving a 2.5 cm/1 in border. Brush the dough between the spoonfuls of filling with egg white.

Cutting out lasagne
Take a sheet of pasta dough and cut out neat rectangles about 18 x 7.5 cm/7 x 3 in to make sheets of lasagne. Lay on a clean dish towel to dry.

2 Lay a second sheet of pasta carefully over the top. Press around each mound of filling, excluding any air pockets.

3 Using a fluted pastry wheel or a sharp knife, cut between the stuffing.

Making pasta bows (farfalle)

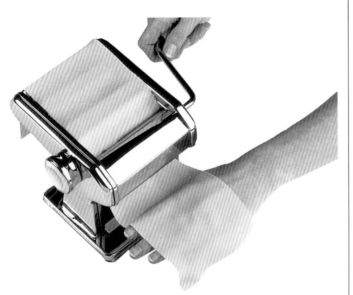

1 Roll the pasta dough through a pasta machine until the sheets are very thin. Then cut into long strips 4 cm/1½ in wide.

2 Cut the strips into small rectangles. Run a pastry wheel along the two shorter edges of the little rectangles – this will give the bows a decorative edge.

3 Moisten the centre of the strips and using a finger and thumb, gently pinch each rectangle together in the middle to make little pasta bows.

Making tagliatelle

1 Lightly flour some spinach-flavoured pasta dough and roll it up into a strip 30 × 10 cm/12 × 4 in.

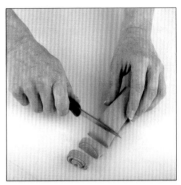

2 Using a sharp knife, cut straight across the roll.

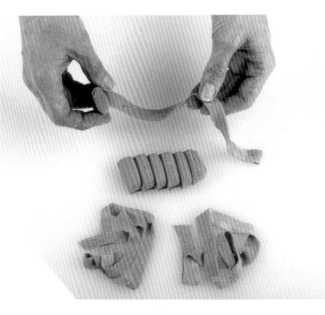

3 Carefully unravel each little roll as you cut it to make ribbons of fresh tagliatelle.

Consommé with Agnolotti

Serves 4–6

INGREDIENTS

75 g/3 oz cooked peeled prawns
75 g/3 oz canned crab meat, drained
5 ml/1 tsp fresh root ginger, peeled
    and finely grated
15 ml/1 tbsp fresh white
    breadcrumbs
5 ml/1 tsp light soy sauce
1 spring onion, finely chopped
1 garlic clove, crushed
1 quantity of basic pasta dough
egg white, beaten
400 g/14 oz can chicken or
    fish consommé
30 ml/2 tbsp sherry or vermouth
salt and ground black pepper
50 g/2 oz cooked, peeled prawns
    and fresh coriander leaves,
    to garnish

prawns

root ginger *crab meat*

spring onion *fresh coriander*

garlic

chicken consommé

flour

fresh white breadcrumbs

basic pasta dough

1 Put the prawns, crab meat, ginger, breadcrumbs, soy sauce, onion, garlic and seasoning into a food processor or blender and process until smooth.

2 Roll the pasta into thin sheets. Stamp out 32 rounds 5 cm/2 in in diameter, with a fluted pastry cutter.

3 Place a small teaspoon of the filling in the centre of half the pasta rounds. Brush the edges of each round with egg white and sandwich with a second round on top. Pinch the edges together firmly to stop the filling seeping out.

4 Cook the pasta in a large pan of boiling, salted water for 5 minutes (cook in batches to stop them sticking together). Remove and drop into a bowl of cold water for 5 seconds before placing on a tray. (You can make these pasta shapes a day in advance. Cover with clear film and store in the fridge.)

5 Heat the chicken or fish consommé in a pan with the sherry or vermouth. When piping hot, add the cooked pasta shapes and simmer for 1–2 minutes.

6 Serve in a shallow soup bowl covered with hot consommé. Garnish with extra peeled prawns and fresh coriander leaves.

NUTRITIONAL NOTES

PER PORTION:

ENERGY 300Kcals/1265KJ **FAT** 4.6g
SATURATED FAT 1.1g **CHOLESTEROL** 148mg
CARBOHYDRATE 43g **FIBRE** 1.7g

Chicken Stellette Soup

Serves 4–6

INGREDIENTS

900 ml/1½ pints/3¾ cups
   chicken stock
1 bay leaf
4 spring onions, sliced
50 g/2oz soup pasta (stellette)
225 g/8 oz button
   mushrooms, sliced
115 g/4 oz cooked chicken breast
150 ml/¼ pint/⅔ cup dry
   white wine
15 ml/1 tbsp chopped parsley
salt and ground black pepper

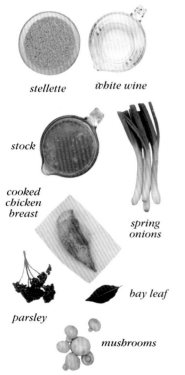

stellette   *white wine*

stock

*cooked
chicken
breast*

*spring
onions*

parsley

bay leaf

mushrooms

1 Put the stock and bay leaf into a pan and bring to the boil.

2 Add the spring onions and mushrooms to the stock.

NUTRITIONAL NOTES
PER PORTION:

ENERGY 126Kcals/529KJ **FAT** 2.2g
SATURATED FAT 0.6g **CHOLESTEROL** 19mg
CARBOHYDRATE 11g **FIBRE** 1.3g

3 Remove the skin from the chicken and slice thinly. Transfer to a plate and set aside.

4 Add the pasta to the pan, cover and simmer for 7–8 minutes. Just before serving, add the chicken, wine and parsley, heat through for 2–3 minutes.

Vegetable Minestrone with Anellini

Serves 6–8

INGREDIENTS
large pinch of saffron strands
1 onion, chopped
1 leek, sliced
1 stick celery, sliced
2 carrots, diced
2–3 garlic cloves, crushed
600 ml/1 pint/2½ cups
    chicken stock
2 x 400 g/14 oz cans
    chopped tomatoes
50 g/2 oz/½ cup frozen peas
50 g/2 oz soup pasta (anellini)
5 ml/1 tsp caster sugar
15 ml/1 tbsp chopped fresh parsley
15 ml/1 tbsp chopped fresh basil
salt and ground black pepper

anellini   *frozen peas*   *onion*

saffron strands   *basil*   *stock*

parsley

chopped tomatoes

carrot   *celery*

garlic   *leek*

1 Soak the pinch of saffron strands in 15 ml/1 tbsp boiling water. Leave to stand for 10 minutes.

2 Meanwhile, put the prepared onion, leek, celery, carrots and garlic into a pan. Add the chicken stock, bring to the boil, cover and simmer for 10 minutes.

NUTRITIONAL NOTES
PER PORTION:

ENERGY 87Kcals/367KJ **FAT** 0.7g
SATURATED FAT 0.1g **CHOLESTEROL** 0mg
CARBOHYDRATE 17g **FIBRE** 3.3g

3 Add the canned tomatoes, the saffron with its liquid, and the peas. Bring back to the boil and add the anellini. Simmer for 10 minutes until tender.

4 Season with salt, pepper and sugar to taste. Stir in the chopped herbs just before serving.

Beetroot Soup with Ravioli

Serves 4–6

INGREDIENTS
1 quantity of basic pasta dough
egg white, beaten, for brushing
flour, for dusting
1 small onion or shallot,
    finely chopped
2 garlic cloves, crushed
5 ml/1 tsp fennel seeds
600 ml/1 pint/2½ cups chicken or
    vegetable stock
225 g/8 oz cooked beetroot
30 ml/2 tbsp fresh orange juice
fennel or dill leaves, to garnish
crusty bread, to serve

FOR THE FILLING
115 g/4 oz mushrooms,
    finely chopped
1 shallot or small onion,
    finely chopped
1–2 garlic cloves, crushed
5 ml/1 tsp fresh thyme
15 ml/1 tbsp fresh parsley
90 ml/6 tbsp fresh white
    breadcrumbs
salt and ground black pepper
large pinch ground nutmeg

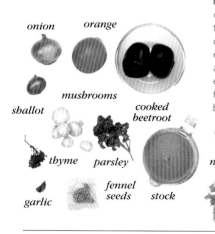

onion   orange

mushrooms

shallot   cooked beetroot

thyme   parsley

garlic   fennel seeds   stock   nutmeg

dill   basic pasta dough   breadcrumbs

1 Process all the filling ingredients in a food processor or blender.

2 Roll the pasta into thin sheets. Lay one piece over a ravioli tray and put a teaspoonful of the filling into each depression. Brush around the edges of each ravioli with egg white. Cover with another sheet of pasta and press the edges well together to seal. Transfer to a floured dish towel and rest for 1 hour before cooking.

3 Cook the ravioli in a large pan of boiling, salted water for 2 minutes. (Cook in batches to stop them sticking together.) Remove and drop into a bowl of cold water for 5 seconds before placing on a tray. (You can make these pasta shapes a day in advance. Cover with clear film and store in the fridge.) Put the onion, garlic and fennel seeds into a pan with 150 ml/¼ pint/⅔ cup of the stock. Bring to the boil, cover and simmer for 5 minutes until tender. Peel and finely dice the beetroot (reserve 60 ml/4 tbsp for the garnish). Add the rest to the soup with the remaining stock. and bring to the boil.

4 Add the orange juice and cooked ravioli and simmer for 2 minutes. Serve in shallow soup bowls, garnished with the reserved, diced beetroot and fennel or dill leaves. Serve hot, with some crusty bread.

NUTRITIONAL NOTES
PER PORTION:

ENERGY 358Kcals/1504KJ **FAT** 4.9g
SATURATED FAT 1.0g **CHOLESTEROL** 110mg
CARBOHYDRATE 67g **FIBRE** 4.3g

Sweetcorn Chowder with Conchigliette

Serves 6–8

INGREDIENTS
1 small green pepper
450 g/1 lb potatoes, peeled
    and diced
350 g/12 oz/2 cups canned or
    frozen sweetcorn
1 onion, chopped
1 stick celery, chopped
a bouquet garni (bay leaf, parsley
    stalks and thyme)
600 ml/1 pint/2½ cups
    chicken stock
300 ml/½ pint/1¼ cups
    skimmed milk
50 g/2 oz small pasta shells
    (conchigliette)
150 g/5 oz smoked turkey
    rashers, diced
bread sticks, to serve
salt and ground black pepper

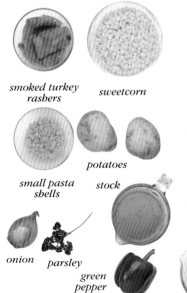

smoked turkey
rashers

sweetcorn

potatoes

small pasta
shells

stock

onion   parsley

green
pepper

celery

bay leaf   thyme

skimmed
milk

1 Halve the green pepper, remove the stalk and seeds. Cut the flesh into small dice, cover with boiling water and stand for 2 minutes. Drain and rinse.

2 Put the potatoes into a saucepan with the sweetcorn, onion, celery, green pepper, bouquet garni and stock. Bring to the boil, cover and simmer for 20 minutes until tender.

3 Add the milk, and season with salt and pepper. Process half of the soup in a food processor or blender and return to the pan with the conchigliette. Simmer for 10 minutes.

4 Fry the turkey rashers quickly in a non-stick frying pan for 2–3 minutes. Stir into the soup. Serve with bread sticks.

NUTRITIONAL NOTES
PER PORTION:

ENERGY 215Kcals/904KJ **FAT** 1.6g
SATURATED FAT 0.3g **CHOLESTEROL** 13mg
CARBOHYDRATE 41g **FIBRE** 2.8g

Pasta Bonbons

Serves 4–6

INGREDIENTS
1 quantity of basic pasta dough
flour, for dusting
egg white, beaten
salt and pepper

FILLING
1 small onion, finely chopped
1 garlic clove, crushed
150 ml/¼ pint/⅔ cup chicken stock
225 g/8 oz minced turkey meat
2–3 fresh sage leaves, chopped
2 canned anchovy fillets, drained

SAUCE
150 ml/¼ pint/⅔ cup chicken stock
200 g/7 oz low-fat cream cheese
15 ml/1 tbsp lemon juice
5 ml/1 tsp caster sugar
2 tomatoes, skinned, seeded and
    finely diced
½ purple onion, finely chopped
6 small cornichons (pickled
    gherkins), sliced

1 To make the filling, put the onion, garlic and stock into a pan. Bring to the boil, cover and simmer for 5 minutes until tender. Uncover and boil for about 5 minutes or until the stock has reduced to 30 ml/2 tbsp.

2 Add the minced turkey, and stir over the heat until no longer pink in colour. Add the sage and anchovy fillets and season with salt and pepper. Cook uncovered for 5 minutes until all the liquid has been absorbed. Leave to cool.

3 Divide the pasta dough in half. Roll into thin sheets and cut into 9 x 6 cm/3½ x 2½ in rectangles. Lay on a lightly floured dish towel and repeat with the remaining dough.

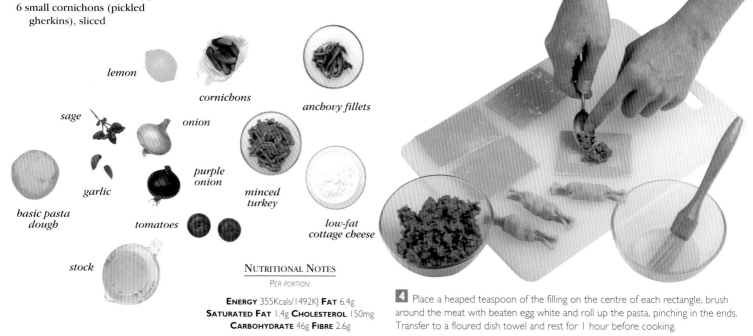

lemon

cornichons

anchovy fillets

sage

onion

garlic

purple onion

minced turkey

basic pasta dough

tomatoes

low-fat cottage cheese

stock

NUTRITIONAL NOTES

PER PORTION:

ENERGY 355Kcals/1492KJ FAT 6.4g
SATURATED FAT 1.4g CHOLESTEROL 150mg
CARBOHYDRATE 46g FIBRE 2.6g

4 Place a heaped teaspoon of the filling on the centre of each rectangle, brush around the meat with beaten egg white and roll up the pasta, pinching in the ends. Transfer to a floured dish towel and rest for 1 hour before cooking.

5 To make the sauce, put the stock, cream cheese, lemon juice and sugar into a pan. Heat gently and whisk until smooth. Add the diced tomatoes, onion and cornichons.

6 Cook the pasta in a large pan of boiling, salted water for 5 minutes. (Cook in batches to stop them sticking together). Remove with a slotted spoon, drain well and drop into the sauce. Repeat until all the bonbons are cooked. Simmer for 2–3 minutes. Serve in pasta bowls or soup plates and spoon over a little sauce.

Spinach Tagliarini with Asparagus

Serves 4–6

INGREDIENTS

2 chicken breasts, skinned
    and boned
15 ml/1 tbsp light soy sauce
30 ml/2 tbsp sherry
30 ml/2 tbsp cornflour
8 spring onions, trimmed and cut
    into 2.5 cm/1 in diagonal slices
1–2 garlic cloves, crushed
needle shreds of rind of half a
    lemon and 30 ml/2 tbsp
    lemon juice
150 ml/¼ pint/⅔ cup chicken stock
5 ml/1 tsp caster sugar
225 g/8 oz slender asparagus spears,
    cut in 7.5 cm/3 in lengths
1 quantity of basic pasta dough,
    with 115 g/4 oz cooked, pressed
    spinach added, or 450 g/1 lb
    fresh tagliarini pasta
salt and ground black pepper

spring onions

asparagus

garlic

lemon

chicken breasts

soy sauce

basic pasta dough

stock

1 Place the chicken breasts between two sheets of clear film and flatten to a thickness of 5 mm/¼ in with a rolling-pin.

2 Cut into 2.5 cm/1 in strips across the grain of the fillets. Put the chicken into a bowl with the soy sauce, sherry, cornflour and seasoning. Toss to coat each piece.

NUTRITIONAL NOTES
PER PORTION:

ENERGY 369Kcals/1548KJ **FAT** 6.9g
SATURATED FAT 1.8g **CHOLESTEROL** 142mg
CARBOHYDRATE 50g **FIBRE** 3.4g

3 In a large non-stick frying pan, put the chicken, spring onions, garlic and needle shreds of lemon rind. Add the stock and bring to the boil, stirring constantly until thickened. Add the sugar, lemon juice and asparagus. Simmer for 4-5 minutes until tender.

4 Meanwhile cook the pasta in a large pan of boiling, salted water for 2–3 minutes. Drain thoroughly. Arrange on serving plates and spoon over the chicken and asparagus sauce. Serve the dish immediately.

Sweet and Sour Peppers with Bows

Serves 4–6

INGREDIENTS

1 red, 1 yellow and 1 orange pepper
1 garlic clove, crushed
30 ml/2 tbsp capers
30 ml/2 tbsp raisins
5 ml/1 tsp wholegrain mustard
rind and juice of 1 lime
5 ml/1 tsp runny honey
30 ml/2 tbsp chopped
    fresh coriander
225 g/8 oz pasta bows (farfalle)
salt and ground black pepper
shavings of Parmesan cheese,
    to serve (optional)

raisins

red pepper

yellow pepper

coriander

orange pepper

pasta bows

Parmesan cheese

honey

garlic

capers

1 Quarter the peppers, remove the stalk and seeds. Put into boiling water and cook for 10–15 minutes until tender. Drain and rinse under cold water. Peel away the skin and cut the flesh into strips lengthways.

2 Put the garlic, capers, raisins, mustard, lime rind and juice, honey, coriander and seasoning into a bowl and whisk together.

3 Cook the pasta in a large pan of boiling, salted water for 10–12 minutes until tender. Drain thoroughly.

4 Return the pasta to the pan, add the reserved peppers and dressing. Heat gently and toss to mix. Transfer to a warm serving bowl. Serve with a few shavings of Parmesan cheese, if using.

NUTRITIONAL NOTES

PER PORTION:

ENERGY 268Kcals/1125KJ **FAT** 2.0g
SATURATED FAT 0.5g **CHOLESTEROL** 1.3mg
CARBOHYDRATE 57g **FIBRE** 4.3g

Herb Pasta Crescents

Serves 4–6

INGREDIENTS
1 quantity of basic pasta dough,
   with 45 ml/3 tbsp chopped fresh
   herbs added
egg white, beaten, for brushing
flour, for dusting
basil leaves, to garnish

FILLING
225 g/8 oz frozen chopped spinach
1 small onion, finely chopped
pinch of ground nutmeg
115 g/4 oz low-fat cottage cheese
1 egg, beaten
25 g/1 oz Parmesan cheese
salt and ground black pepper

SAUCE
300 ml/¹/₂ pint/1¹/₄ cups
   skimmed milk
25 g/1 oz sunflower margarine
45 ml/3 tbsp plain flour
1.5 ml/¹/₄ tsp ground nutmeg
30 ml/2 tbsp chopped fresh herbs
   (chives, basil and parsley)

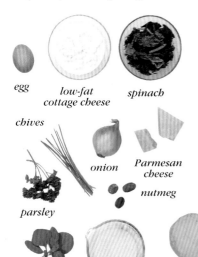

egg

low-fat
cottage cheese

spinach

chives

onion

Parmesan
cheese

nutmeg

parsley

basil

skimmed milk

basic pasta
dough

margarine

1 To make the filling, put the spinach and onion into a pan, cover and cook slowly to defrost. Remove the lid, increase the heat to drive off any water Season with salt, pepper and nutmeg. Turn the spinach into a bowl and cool slightly. Add the cottage cheese, beaten egg and Parmesan cheese.

2 Roll the herb pasta into thin sheets. Cut into 7.5 cm/3 in rounds with a fluted pastry cutter.

3 Place a dessertspoon of filling in the centre of each round. Brush the edges with egg white. Fold each in half (to make crescents). Press the edges together to seal. Transfer to a floured dish towel and rest for 1 hour before cooking the pasta.

4 Put all the sauce ingredients (except the herbs) into a pan. With a sauce whisk, thicken over a medium heat until smooth. Season with salt, pepper and nutmeg to taste. Stir in the herbs.

5 Cook the pasta in a large pan of boiling, salted water for 3 minutes (cook in batches to stop them sticking together). Drain thoroughly.

6 Put the crescents on to warmed serving plates and pour over the herb sauce. Garnish with basil leaves and serve at once.

NUTRITIONAL NOTES
PER PORTION:

ENERGY 421Kcals/1768KJ **FAT** 14g
SATURATED FAT 3.8g **CHOLESTEROL** 184mg
CARBOHYDRATE 54g **FIBRE** 3.6g

CLASSIC PASTA DISHES

Lasagne

Serves 6–'8

INGREDIENTS
1 large onion, chopped
2 garlic cloves, crushed
500 g/1¼ lb minced turkey meat
450 g/1 lb carton passata (smooth, thick, sieved tomatoes)
5 ml/1 tsp mixed dried herbs
225 g/8 oz frozen leaf spinach, defrosted
200 g/7 oz lasagne verdi
200 g/7 oz low-fat cottage cheese

SAUCE
25 g/1 oz low-fat margarine
25 g/1 oz plain flour
300 ml/½ pint/1¼ cups skimmed milk
1.5 ml/¼ tsp ground nutmeg
25 g/1 oz grated Parmesan cheese
salt and ground black pepper
mixed salad, to serve

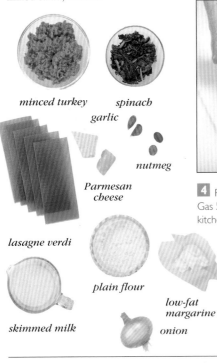

minced turkey *spinach*

garlic

nutmeg

Parmesan cheese

lasagne verdi

plain flour

skimmed milk

low-fat margarine

onion

low-fat cottage cheese

passata

1 Put the onion, garlic and minced turkey into a non-stick saucepan. Brown quickly for 5 minutes, stirring with a wooden spoon to separate the pieces.

2 Add the sieved tomatoes, herbs and seasoning. Bring to the boil, cover and simmer for 30 minutes.

3 For the sauce: put all the sauce ingredients, except the Parmesan cheese, into a saucepan. Heat to thicken, whisking constantly until bubbling and smooth. Adjust the seasoning, add the cheese to the sauce and stir.

4 Preheat the oven to 190°C/375°F/ Gas 5. Lay the spinach leaves out on kitchen paper and pat dry.

5 Layer the turkey mixture, dried lasagne, cottage cheese and spinach in a 2 litre/3½ pint/8 cup ovenproof dish, starting and ending with a layer of turkey.

6 Spoon the sauce over the top to cover and bake for 45-50 minutes or until bubbling. Serve with a mixed salad.

NUTRITIONAL NOTES
PER PORTION:

ENERGY 351Kcals/1472KJ **FAT** 6.0g
SATURATED FAT 1.7g **CHOLESTEROL** 52mg
CARBOHYDRATE 40g **FIBRE** 3g

Macaroni Cheese

Serves 4

INGREDIENTS
1 medium onion, chopped
150 ml/¼ pint/⅔ cup vegetable or
  chicken stock
25 g/1 oz low-fat margarine
40 g/1½ oz plain flour
300 ml/½ pint/¼ cup skimmed milk
50 g/2 oz reduced-fat Cheddar
  cheese, grated
5 ml/1 tsp mustard
225 g/8 oz quick-cook macaroni
4 smoked turkey rashers, cut in half
2–3 firm tomatoes, sliced
a few fresh basil leaves
15 ml/1 tbsp grated Parmesan
  cheese
salt and ground black pepper

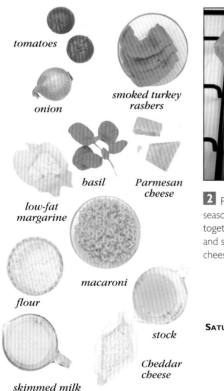

tomatoes

onion

smoked turkey
rashers

basil

Parmesan
cheese

low-fat
margarine

macaroni

flour

stock

skimmed milk

Cheddar
cheese

1 Put the onion and stock into a non-stick frying pan. Bring to the boil, stirring occasionally and cook for 5–6 minutes or until the stock has reduced entirely and the onions are transparent.

2 Put the margarine, flour, milk, and seasoning into a saucepan and whisk together over the heat until thickened and smooth. Draw aside and add the cheese, mustard and onions.

NUTRITIONAL NOTES
PER PORTION:

ENERGY 152Kcals/637KJ **FAT** 2.8g
SATURATED FAT 0.7g **CHOLESTEROL** 12mg
CARBOHYDRATE 23g **FIBRE** 1.1g

3 Cook the macaroni in a large pan of boiling, salted water for 6 minutes or according to the instructions on the packet. Drain thoroughly and stir into the sauce. Transfer the macaroni to a shallow ovenproof dish.

4 Arrange the turkey rashers and tomatoes so that they overlap on top of the macaroni cheese. Tuck the basil leaves over the tomatoes. Lightly sprinkle with Parmesan cheese and grill to lightly brown the top.

Spaghetti Bolognese

Serves 8

INGREDIENTS

1 medium onion, chopped
2–3 garlic cloves, crushed
300 ml/½ pint/1¼ cups beef or
 chicken stock
450 g/1 lb extra lean minced turkey
 or beef
2 x 400 g/14 oz cans
 chopped tomatoes
5 ml/1 tsp dried basil
5 ml/1 tsp dried oregano
60 ml/4 tbsp concentrated
 tomato purée
450 g/1 lb button mushrooms,
 quartered or sliced
150 ml/¼ pint/⅔ cup red wine
450 g/1 lb spaghetti
salt and ground black pepper

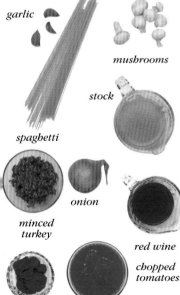

garlic

mushrooms

stock

spaghetti

onion

minced turkey

red wine

chopped tomatoes

tomato purée

1 Put the chopped onion and garlic into a non-stick pan with half of the stock. Bring to the boil and cook for 5 minutes until the onions are tender and the stock has reduced completely.

2 Add the turkey or beef and cook for 5 minutes breaking the meat up with a fork. Add the tomatoes, herbs and tomato purée, bring to the boil, cover and simmer for about 1 hour.

NUTRITIONAL NOTES
PER PORTION:

ENERGY 321Kcals/1350KJ **FAT** 4.1g
SATURATED FAT 1.3g **CHOLESTEROL** 33mg
CARBOHYDRATE 49g **FIBRE** 3.7g

3 Meanwhile put the mushrooms into a non-stick pan with the wine, bring to the boil and cook for 5 minutes or until the wine has evaporated. Add the mushrooms to the meat.

4 Cook the pasta in a large pan of boiling, salted water for 8–10 minutes until tender. Drain thoroughly. Serve topped with meat sauce.

Cannelloni

Serves 4

INGREDIENTS
2 garlic cloves, crushed
2 x 400 g/14 oz cans
   chopped tomatoes
10 ml/2 tsp soft brown sugar
15 ml/1 tbsp fresh basil
15 ml/1 tbsp fresh marjoram
450 g/1 lb frozen chopped spinach
large pinch ground nutmeg
115 g/4 oz cooked lean
   ham, minced
200 g/7 oz low-fat cottage cheese
12–14 cannelloni tubes
50 g/2 oz low-fat mozzarella
   cheese, diced
25 g/1 oz strong Cheddar
   cheese, grated
25 g/1 oz fresh white breadcrumbs
salt and ground black pepper
flat-leaf parsley, to garnish

1 To make the sauce put the garlic, canned tomatoes, sugar and herbs into a pan, bring to the boil and cook, uncovered, for 30 minutes, stirring occasionally, until fairly thick.

2 To make the filling put the spinach into a pan, cover and cook slowly until defrosted. Break up with a fork, then increase the heat to drive off any water. Season with salt, pepper and nutmeg. Turn the spinach into a bowl, cool slightly, then add the minced ham and cottage cheese.

3 Pipe the filling into each tube of uncooked cannelloni. It is easiest to hold them upright with one end flat on a chopping board, while piping from the other end.

Cheddar cheese

breadcrumbs

spinach

mozzarella cheese

cannelloni tubes

low-fat cottage cheese

chopped tomatoes

basil

cooked ham

garlic

nutmeg

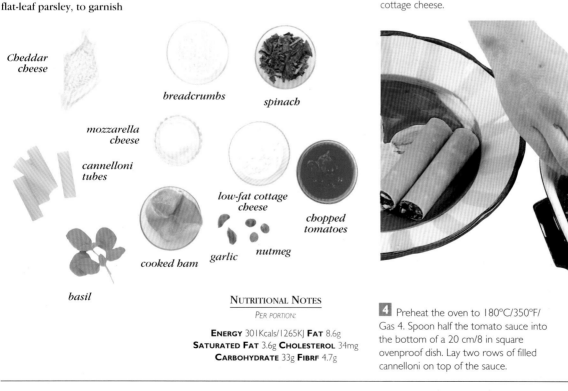

4 Preheat the oven to 180°C/350°F/Gas 4. Spoon half the tomato sauce into the bottom of a 20 cm/8 in square ovenproof dish. Lay two rows of filled cannelloni on top of the sauce.

NUTRITIONAL NOTES
PER PORTION:

ENERGY 301Kcals/1265KJ **FAT** 8.6g
SATURATED FAT 3.6g **CHOLESTEROL** 34mg
CARBOHYDRATE 33g **FIBRF** 4.7g

5 Scatter over the diced mozzarella and cover with the rest of the sauce.

6 Sprinkle over the Cheddar cheese and breadcrumbs. Bake in a preheated oven for 30–40 minutes. Grill the top to brown, if necessary. Garnish with flat leaf parsley.

Ravioli (with Bolognese Sauce)

Serves 6

INGREDIENTS

225 g/8 oz low-fat cottage cheese
30 ml/2 tbsp grated Parmesan
   cheese, plus extra for serving
1 egg white, beaten, including extra
   for brushing
1.5 ml/¼ tsp ground nutmeg
1 quantity of basic pasta dough
flour, for dusting
1 medium onion, finely chopped
1 garlic clove, crushed
150 ml/¼ pint/⅔ cup beef stock
350 g/12 oz minced extra lean beef
120 ml/4 fl oz/½ cup red wine
30 ml/2 tbsp concentrated
   tomato purée
400 g/14 oz can chopped tomatoes
2.5 ml/½ tsp chopped
   fresh rosemary
1.5 ml/¼ tsp ground allspice
salt and ground black pepper

nutmeg

onion   minced beef   stock

tomato
purée   low-fat
cottage cheese   red wine

Parmesan
cheese   chopped
tomatoes

rosemary
egg

garlic

1 To make the filling mix the cottage cheese, grated Parmesan, egg white, seasoning and nutmeg together thoroughly.

2 Roll the pasta into thin sheets, place a small teaspoon of filling along the pasta in rows 5 cm/2 in apart.

3 Moisten between the filling with beaten egg white. Lay a second sheet of pasta lightly over the top and press between each pocket to remove any air and seal firmly.

4 Cut into rounds with a fluted ravioli or pastry cutter. Transfer to a floured cloth and rest for at least 30 minutes before cooking.

5 To make the Bolognese sauce cook the onion and garlic in the stock for 5 minutes or until all the stock has reduced. Add the beef and cook quickly to brown, breaking up the meat with a fork. Add the wine, tomato purée, chopped tomatoes, rosemary and allspice, bring to the boil and simmer for 1 hour. Adjust the seasoning to taste.

6 Cook the ravioli in a large pan of boiling, salted water for 4–5 minutes. (Cook in batches to stop them sticking together). Drain thoroughly. Serve topped with Bolognese sauce. Serve grated Parmesan cheese separately.

NUTRITIONAL NOTES
PER PORTION:

ENERGY 321Kcals/1347KJ **FAT** 8.8g
SATURATED FAT 3.1g **CHOLESTEROL** 158mg
CARBOHYDRATE 32g **FIBRE** 2g

Spaghetti alla Carbonara

Serves 4

INGREDIENTS

150 g/5 oz smoked turkey rashers
1 medium onion, chopped
1–2 garlic cloves, crushed
150 ml/¼ pint/⅔ cup chicken stock
150 ml/¼ pint/⅔ cup dry
    white wine
200 g/7 oz low-fat cream cheese
450 g/1 lb chilli and garlic-
    flavoured spaghetti
30 ml/2 tbsp chopped fresh parsley
salt and ground black pepper
shavings of Parmesan cheese,
    to serve

garlic

*flavoured
spaghetti*

parsley

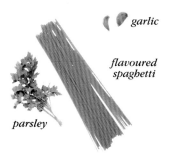
*smoked turkey
rashers*

*low-fat cream
cheese*

onion

white wine

stock

1 Cut the turkey rashers into 1 cm/½ in strips. Fry quickly in a non-stick pan for 2–3 minutes. Add the onion, garlic and stock to the pan. Bring to the boil, cover and simmer for 5 minutes until tender.

2 Add the wine and boil rapidly until reduced by half. Whisk in the cream cheese until smooth.

3 Meanwhile cook the spaghetti in a large pan of boiling, salted water for 10–12 minutes. Drain thoroughly.

4 Return to the pan with the sauce and parsley, toss well and serve immediately with shavings of Parmesan cheese.

NUTRITIONAL NOTES
PER PORTION:

ENERGY 500Kcals/2102KJ **FAT** 3.3g
SATURATED FAT 0.5g **CHOLESTEROL** 21mg
CARBOHYDRATE 89g **FIBRE** 4g

Pasta Shells with Tomato and Tuna Sauce

Serves 6

INGREDIENTS

1 medium onion, finely chopped
1 stick celery, finely chopped
1 red pepper, seeded and diced
1 garlic clove, crushed
150 ml/^{1}/$_4$ pint/^{2}/$_3$ cup chicken stock
400 g/14 oz can chopped tomatoes
15 ml/1 tbsp tomato purée
10 ml/2 tsp caster sugar
15 ml/1 tbsp chopped fresh basil
15 ml/1 tbsp chopped fresh parsley
450 g/1 lb dried pasta shells
400 g/14 oz canned tuna in
    brine, drained
30 ml/2 tbsp capers in
    vinegar, drained
salt and ground black pepper

celery

canned tuna

tomato purée

capers

garlic

red pepper

stock

onion

chopped tomatoes

basil

parsley

1 Put the chopped onion, celery, pepper and garlic into a non-stick pan. Add the stock, bring to the boil and cook for 5 minutes or until the stock has reduced almost completely.

2 Add the tomatoes, tomato purée, sugar and herbs. Season to taste and bring to the boil. Simmer for 30 minutes until thick, stirring occasionally.

NUTRITIONAL NOTES

PER PORTION:

ENERGY 369Kcals/1549KJ **FAT** 2.1g
SATURATED FAT 0.4g **CHOLESTEROL** 34mg
CARBOHYDRATE 65g **FIBRE** 4g

3 Meanwhile cook the pasta in a large pan of boiling, salted water according to packet instructions. Drain thoroughly and transfer to a warm serving dish.

4 Flake the tuna fish into large chunks and add to the sauce with the capers. Heat gently for 1–2 minutes, pour over the pasta, toss gently and serve at once.

Tortellini

Serves 6–8 as a starter or 4–6 as a main course

INGREDIENTS
115 g/4oz smoked, lean ham
115 g/4 oz chicken breast, boned
   and skinned
900 ml/1½ pint/3¾ cups chicken or
   vegetable stock
coriander stalks
30 ml/2 tbsp grated Parmesan
   cheese, plus extra for serving
1 egg, beaten, plus egg white
   for brushing
30 ml/2 tbsp chopped
   fresh coriander
1 quantity of basic pasta dough
flour, for dusting
salt and ground black pepper
coriander leaves, to garnish

*basic pasta
dough*

*smoked
ham*

*chicken
breast*

*grated Parmesan
cheese*

stock

*fresh
coriander*

egg

1 Cut the ham and chicken into large chunks and put them into a saucepan with 150 ml/¼ pint/⅔ cup of the chicken or vegetable stock and some coriander stalks. Bring to the boil, cover and simmer for 20 minutes until tender. Cool slightly in the stock.

2 Drain the ham and chicken and mince finely (reserve the stock). Put into a bowl with the Parmesan cheese, beaten egg, chopped coriander and season with salt and pepper.

3 Roll the pasta into thin sheets, cut into 4 cm/1½ in squares. Put 2.5 ml/½ tsp of filling on each. Brush edges with egg white and fold each square into a triangle; press out any air and seal firmly.

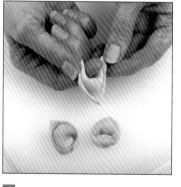

4 Curl each triangle around the tip of a forefinger and press the two ends together firmly.

5 Lay on a lightly floured tea towel to rest for 30 minutes before cooking.

NUTRITIONAL NOTES
PER PORTION:

ENERGY 335Kcal/1405KJ **FAT** 9.7g
SATURATED FAT 3.6g **CHOLESTEROL** 193mg
CARBOHYDRATE 39g **FIBRE** 1.6g

6 Strain the reserved stock and add to the remainder. Put into a pan and bring to the boil. Lower the heat to a gentle boil and add the tortellini. Cook for 5 minutes. Then turn off the heat, cover the pan and stand for 20–30 minutes. Serve in soup plates with some of the stock, garnish with coriander leaves. Serve grated Parmesan separately.

Penne with Salmon and Dill

Serves 6

INGREDIENTS

350 g/12 oz fresh salmon
    fillet, skinned
115 g/4 oz sliced smoked salmon
1–2 shallots, finely chopped
115 g/4 oz button mushrooms,
    quartered
150 ml/¼ pint/⅔ cup light red or
    rosé wine
150 ml/¼ pint/⅔ cup fish stock
150 ml/¼ pint/⅔ cup low-fat
    crème fraîche
30 ml/2 tbsp chopped fresh dill
350 g/12 oz penne
salt and ground black pepper
sprigs of dill, to garnish

1 Cut the fresh salmon into 2.5 cm/
1 in cubes. Cut the smoked salmon into
1 cm/½ in strips.

2 Put the shallots and mushrooms into
a non-stick pan with the red or rosé
wine. Bring to the boil and cook for
about 5 minutes or until the wine has
reduced almost completely.

3 Add the fish stock and crème fraîche
and stir until smooth. Then add the fresh
salmon, cover the pan and cook gently
for 2–3 minutes.

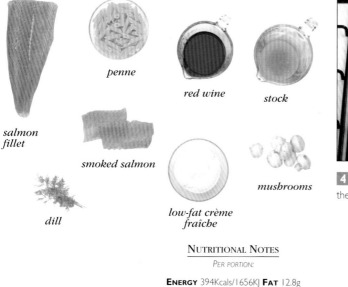

penne

red wine

stock

salmon fillet

smoked salmon

low-fat crème fraîche

mushrooms

dill

4 Remove from the heat and stir in
the chopped dill and seasoning.

5 Meanwhile cook the pasta in a large
pan of boiling, salted water according to
the instructions on the packet. Drain
thoroughly and transfer to a warm
serving dish. Add the smoked salmon to
the sauce and pour over the pasta. Toss
lightly to mix. Serve at once, garnished
with sprigs of dill.

NUTRITIONAL NOTES

PER PORTION:

ENERGY 394Kcals/1656KJ **FAT** 12.8g
SATURATED FAT 4.6g **CHOLESTEROL** 64mg
CARBOHYDRATE 45g **FIBRE** 2g

Prawn and Pasta Salad with Green Dressing

Serves 4–6

INGREDIENTS

4 anchovy fillets, drained
60 ml/4 tbsp skimmed milk
225 g/8 oz squid
15 ml/1 tbsp chopped capers
15 ml/1 tbsp chopped gherkins
1–2 garlic cloves, crushed
150 ml/¼ pint/⅔ cup low-fat
    plain yogurt
30–45 ml/2–3 tbsp reduced-fat
    mayonnaise
squeeze of lemon juice
50 g/2 oz watercress, chopped finely
30 ml/2 tbsp chopped fresh parsley
30 ml/2 tbsp chopped fresh basil
350 g/12 oz fusilli
350 g/12 oz shelled prawns
salt and ground black pepper

squid *anchovy fillets*
capers and gherkins
watercress
parsley
low-fat plain yogurt
prawns
fusilli *reduced-fat mayonnaise*
garlic *lemon* *basil*

1 Put the anchovies into a small bowl and cover with the skimmed milk. Leave to soak for 10 minutes to remove the oil and strong salty flavour. Pull the head from the body of each squid and remove the quill. Peel outer speckled skin from the bodies. Cut the tentacles from the heads and rinse under cold water. Cut into 5 mm/¼ in rings.

2 To make the dressing, mix the capers, gherkins, garlic, yogurt, mayonnaise, lemon juice and fresh herbs in a bowl. Drain and chop the anchovies. Add to the dressing with the seasoning.

3 Drop the squid rings into a large pan of boiling, salted water. Lower the heat and simmer for 1–2 minutes (do not overcook or the squid will become tough). Remove with a slotted spoon. Cook the pasta in the same water according to the instructions on the packet. Drain thoroughly.

4 Mix the prawns and squid into the dressing in a large bowl. Add the pasta, toss and serve warm or cold as a salad.

NUTRITIONAL NOTES

PER PORTION:

ENERGY 502Kcals/2107KJ **FAT** 6.9g
SATURATED FAT 1.1g **CHOLESTEROL** 72mg
CARBOHYDRATE 71g **FIBRE** 3.2g

Crab Pasta Salad with Spicy Cocktail Dressing

Serves 6

INGREDIENTS
350 g/12 oz fusilli
1 small red pepper, seeded and
    finely chopped
2 x 175 g/6 oz cans white crab
    meat, drained
115 g/4 oz cherry tomatoes, halved
1/4 cucumber, halved, seeded and
    sliced into crescents
15 ml/1 tbsp lemon juice
300 ml/1/2 pint/1 1/4 cups
    low-fat yogurt
2 sticks celery, finely chopped
10 ml/2 tsp horseradish cream
2.5 ml/1/2 tsp ground paprika
2.5 ml/1/2 tsp Dijon mustard
30 ml/2 tbsp sweet tomato pickle
    or chutney
salt and ground black pepper
fresh basil, to garnish

celery

paprika

lemon

red pepper   *fusilli*

cucumber

crab meat

cherry tomatoes

low-fat yogurt

horseradish cream

tomato pickle

1 Cook the pasta in a large pan of boiling, salted water according to the instructions on the packet. Drain and rinse thoroughly under cold water.

2 Cover the chopped red pepper with boiling water and stand for 1 minute. Drain and rinse under cold water. Pat dry on kitchen paper.

NUTRITIONAL NOTES
Per portion:

ENERGY 305Kcals/1283KJ **FAT** 2.5g
SATURATED FAT 0.5g **CHOLESTEROL** 43mg
CARBOHYDRATE 53g **FIBRE** 2.9g

3 Drain the crab meat and pick over carefully for pieces of shell. Put into a bowl with the halved tomatoes and sliced cucumber. Season with salt and pepper and sprinkle with lemon juice.

4 To make the dressing, add the red pepper to the yogurt, celery, horseradish, paprika, mustard and sweet tomato pickle or chutney. Mix the pasta with the dressing and transfer to a serving dish. Spoon the crab mixture on top and garnish with fresh basil.

Hot Spicy Prawns with Campanelle

Serves 4–6

INGREDIENTS

225 g/8 oz tiger prawns, cooked
    and peeled
1–2 garlic cloves, crushed
finely grated rind of 1 lemon
15 ml/1 tbsp lemon juice
1.5 ml/¼ tsp red chilli paste or large
    pinch dried ground chilli
15 ml/1 tbsp light soy sauce
150 g/5 oz smoked turkey rashers
1 shallot or small onion,
    finely chopped
60 ml/4 tbsp white wine
225 g/8 oz campanelle
60 ml/4 tbsp fish stock
4 firm ripe tomatoes, skinned,
    seeded and chopped
30 ml/2 tbsp chopped fresh parsley
salt and ground black pepper

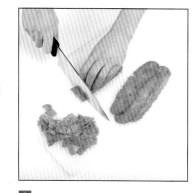

2 Grill the turkey rashers, then cut them into 5 mm/¼ in dice.

1 In a glass bowl, mix the prawns with the garlic, lemon rind and juice, chilli paste or ground chilli and soy sauce. Season with salt and pepper, cover and marinate the prawns for at least 1 hour.

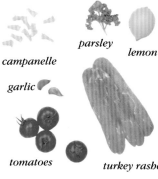

parsley

lemon

campanelle

garlic

tomatoes

turkey rashers

stock

onion

tiger prawns

white wine

soy sauce

3 Put the shallot or onion and white wine into a pan, bring to the boil, cover and cook for 2–3 minutes or until tender and the wine has reduced by half.

4 Cook the campanelle in a large pan of boiling, salted water until *al dente*. Drain thoroughly.

5 Just before serving, put the prawns with their marinade into a large frying pan, bring to the boil quickly and add the smoked turkey and fish stock. Heat through for 1 minute.

6 Add to the pasta with the chopped tomatoes and parsley, toss quickly and serve immediately.

NUTRITIONAL NOTES

PER PORTION:

ENERGY 331Kcals/1388KJ **FAT** 2.9g
SATURATED FAT 0.6g **CHOLESTEROL** 64mg
CARBOHYDRATE 48g **FIBRE** 3.2g

Smoked Haddock in Parsley Sauce

Serves 4

INGREDIENTS

450 g/1 lb smoked haddock fillet
1 small leek or onion, sliced thickly
300 ml/¹/₂ pint/1¹/₄ cups
   skimmed milk
a bouquet garni (bay leaf, thyme
   and parsley stalks)
25 g/1 oz low-fat margarine
25 g/1 oz plain flour
30 ml/2 tbsp chopped fresh parsley
225 g/8 oz pasta shells
salt and ground black pepper
15 g/¹/₂ oz toasted flaked almonds,
   to serve

leek

haddock fillet

salt

parsley

bay leaves

pepper

pasta shells

skimmed milk

plain flour

low-fat margarine

1 Remove all the skin and any bones from the haddock. Put into a pan with the leek or onion, milk and bouquet garni. Bring to the boil, cover and simmer gently for about 8–10 minutes until the fish flakes easily.

2 Strain, reserving the milk for making the sauce, and discard the bouquet garni.

NUTRITIONAL NOTES

PER PORTION:

ENERGY 405Kcals/1700KJ **FAT** 6.9g
SATURATED FAT 1.0g **CHOLESTEROL** 42mg
CARBOHYDRATE 58g **FIBRE** 3.7g

3 Put the margarine, flour and reserved milk into a pan. Bring to the boil and whisk until smooth. Season and add the fish and leek or onion.

4 Cook the pasta in a large pan of boiling water until *al dente*. Drain thoroughly and stir into the sauce with the chopped parsley. Serve immediately, scattered with almonds.

Fusilli with Smoked Trout

Serves 4–6

INGREDIENTS

2 carrots, cut in julienne sticks
1 leek, cut in julienne sticks
2 sticks celery, cut in julienne sticks
150 ml/¼ pint/⅔ cup
    vegetable stock
225 g/8 oz fresh trout fillets, skinned
    and cut into strips
200 g/7 oz low-fat cream cheese
150 ml/¼ pint/⅔ cup medium sweet
    white wine or fish stock
15 ml/1 tbsp chopped fresh dill
    or fennel
225 g/8 oz long curly fusilli
salt and ground black pepper
dill sprigs, to garnish

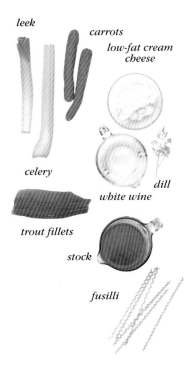

leek
carrots
low-fat cream cheese
celery
dill
white wine
trout fillets
stock
fusilli

1 Put the carrots, leek and celery into a pan with the vegetable stock. Bring to the boil and cook quickly for 4–5 minutes until tender and most of the stock has evaporated. Remove from the heat and add the smoked trout.

2 To make the sauce, put the cream cheese and wine or fish stock into a saucepan, heat and whisk until smooth. Season with salt and pepper. Add the chopped dill or fennel.

NUTRITIONAL NOTES
PER PORTION:

ENERGY 339Kcals/1422KJ **FAT** 4.7g
SATURATED FAT 0.8g **CHOLESTEROL** 57mg
CARBOHYDRATE 49g **FIBRE** 4.1g

3 Cook the fusilli in a large pan of boiling, salted water until *al dente*. Drain thoroughly.

4 Return the fusilli to the pan with the sauce, toss lightly and transfer to a serving bowl. Top with the cooked vegetables and trout. Serve immediately, garnished with dill sprigs.

Saffron Pappardelle

Serves 4

INGREDIENTS
large pinch of saffron strands
4 sun-dried tomatoes, chopped
5 ml/1 tsp fresh thyme
12 large prawns in their shells
225 g/8 oz baby squid
225 g/8 oz monkfish fillet
2–3 garlic cloves, crushed
2 small onions, quartered
1 small bulb fennel, trimmed
    and sliced
150 ml/¼ pint/⅔ cup white wine
225 g/8 oz pappardelle
salt and ground black pepper
30 ml/2 tbsp chopped fresh parsley,
    to garnish

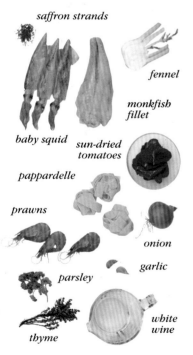

saffron strands

fennel

monkfish fillet

baby squid

sun-dried tomatoes

pappardelle

prawns

onion

garlic

parsley

white wine

thyme

1 Put the saffron, sun-dried tomatoes and thyme into a bowl with 60 ml/4 tbsp hot water. Leave to soak for 30 minutes.

2 Wash the prawns and carefully remove the shells, leaving the heads and tails intact. Pull the head from the body of each squid and remove the quill. Cut the tentacles from the head and rinse under cold water. Pull off the outer skin and cut into 5 mm/¼ in rings. Cut the monkfish into 2.5 cm/1 in cubes.

3 Put the garlic, onions and fennel into a pan with the wine. Cover and simmer for 5 minutes until tender.

4 Add the monkfish, saffron, tomatoes and thyme in their liquid. Cover and cook for 3 minutes. Then add the prawns and squid. Cover and cook gently for 1–2 minutes (do not overcook or the squid will become tough).

5 Meanwhile cook the pasta in a large pan of boiling, salted water until *al dente*. Drain thoroughly.

6 Divide the pasta among four serving dishes and top with the fish and shellfish sauce. Sprinkle with parsley and serve at once.

NUTRITIONAL NOTES
PER PORTION:

ENERGY 381Kcals/1602KJ **FAT** 3.5g
SATURATED FAT 0.6g **CHOLESTEROL** 34mg
CARBOHYDRATE 52g **FIBRE** 3.2g

Sweet and Sour Prawns with Chinese Egg Noodles

Serves 4–6

INGREDIENTS
15 g/¹/₂ oz dried porcini mushrooms
300 ml/¹/₂ pint/1¹/₄ cups hot water
bunch of spring onions, cut into
    thick diagonal slices
2.5 cm/1 in piece of root ginger,
    peeled and grated
1 red pepper, seeded and diced
225 g/8 oz can water
    chestnuts, sliced
45 ml/3 tbsp light soy sauce
30 ml/2 tbsp sherry
350 g/12 oz large peeled prawns
225 g/8 oz Chinese egg noodles

root ginger

red pepper

prawns

spring onions

water chestnuts

egg noodles

soy sauce

porcini mushrooms

1 Put the dried porcini mushrooms into a bowl with the hot water and soak for 15 minutes.

2 Put the spring onions, ginger and diced red pepper into a pan with the mushrooms and their liquid. Bring to the boil, cover and cook for about 5 minutes until tender.

NUTRITIONAL NOTES
PER PORTION:

ENERGY 391Kcals/1640KJ **FAT** 7.1g
SATURATED FAT 0.3g **CHOLESTEROL** 88mg
CARBOHYDRATE 54g **FIBRE** 2.8g

3 Add the water chestnuts, soy sauce, sherry and prawns. Cover and cook gently for 2 minutes.

4 Cook the egg noodles according to the instructions on the packet. Drain thoroughly and transfer to a warmed serving dish. Spoon the hot prawns on top. Serve at once.

Pasta with Scallops in Warm Green Tartare Sauce

Serves 4

INGREDIENTS

120 ml/4 fl oz/½ cup low-fat
  crème fraîche
10 ml/2 tsp wholegrain mustard
2 garlic cloves, crushed
30–45 ml/2–3 tbsp fresh lime juice
60 ml/4 tbsp chopped fresh parsley
30 ml/2 tbsp snipped chives
350 g/12 oz black tagliatelle
12 large scallops
60 ml/4 tbsp white wine
150 ml/¼ pint/⅔ cup fish stock
salt and ground black pepper
lime wedges and parsley sprigs,
  to garnish

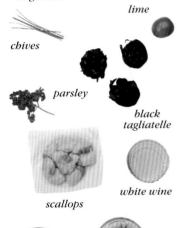

chives

lime

parsley

*black
tagliatelle*

scallops

white wine

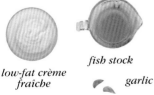

*low-fat crème
fraîche*

fish stock

garlic

1 To make the tartare sauce, mix the crème fraîche, mustard, garlic, lime juice, herbs and seasoning together in a bowl.

2 Cook the pasta in a large pan of boiling, salted water until *al dente*. Drain thoroughly.

NUTRITIONAL NOTES
PER PORTION:

ENERGY 433Kcals/1820KJ **FAT** 3.4g
SATURATED FAT 0.6g **CHOLESTEROL** 45mg
CARBOHYDRATE 68g **FIBRE** 3.4g

3 Slice the scallops in half, horizontally. Keep any coral whole. Put the white wine and fish stock into a saucepan. Heat to simmering point. Add the scallops and cook very gently for 3–4 minutes (no longer or they will become tough).

4 Remove the scallops. Boil the wine and stock to reduce by half and add the green sauce to the pan. Heat gently to warm, replace the scallops and cook for 1 minute. Spoon over the pasta and garnish with lime wedges and parsley.

PASTA WITH MEAT

Rolled Stuffed Cannelloni

Serves 4

INGREDIENTS
12 sheets lasagne
fresh basil leaves, to garnish

FILLING
2–3 garlic cloves, crushed
1 small onion, finely chopped
150 ml/¼ pint/⅔ cup white wine
450 g/1 lb minced turkey
15 ml/1 tbsp dried basil
15 ml/1 tbsp dried thyme
40 g/1½ oz fresh white
   breadcrumbs
salt and ground black pepper

SAUCE
25 g/1 oz low-fat margarine
25 g/1 oz plain flour
300 ml/½ pint/1¼ cups
   skimmed milk
4 sun-dried tomatoes, chopped
15 ml/1 tbsp mixed chopped fresh
   herbs (basil, parsley, marjoram)
30 ml/2 tbsp grated

skimmed milk

sliced
white bread

lasagne

sun-dried
tomatoes

minced
turkey

garlic

parsley

grated
Parmesan
cheese

onion

flour

low-fat
margarine

white
wine

basil

1 Put the garlic, onion and half the wine into a pan. Cover and cook for about 5 minutes until tender. Increase the heat, add the turkey and break up with a wooden spoon. Cook quickly until all the liquid has evaporated and the turkey begins to brown slightly.

2 Lower the heat, add the remaining wine, seasoning and dried herbs. Cover and cook for 20 minutes. Draw off the heat and stir in the breadcrumbs. Leave to cool.

3 Cook the lasagne sheets in a large pan of boiling, salted water until *al dente*. Cook in batches to prevent them sticking together. Drain thoroughly and rinse in cold water. Pat dry on a clean dish towel.

4 Lay the lasagne on a chopping board. Spoon the turkey mixture along one short edge and roll it up to encase the filling. Cut the tubes in half.

5 Preheat the oven to 200°C/400°F/Gas 6. Put the margarine, flour and skimmed milk into a pan, heat and whisk until smooth. Add the chopped tomatoes, fresh herbs and seasoning.

6 Spoon a thin layer of the sauce into a shallow ovenproof dish and arrange a layer of cannelloni on top. Spoon over a layer of sauce and cover with more cannelloni and sauce. Sprinkle with grated Parmesan and bake for 10–15 minutes until lightly browned. Serve at once, garnished with fresh basil leaves.

NUTRITIONAL NOTES
PER PORTION:

ENERGY 336Kcals/1411KJ **FAT** 7.4g
SATURATED FAT 2.7g **CHOLESTEROL** 65mg
CARBOHYDRATE 26g **FIBRE** 1.4g

Chilli Mince and Pipe Rigate

Serves 6

INGREDIENTS

450 g/1 lb extra lean minced beef
  or turkey
1 onion, finely chopped
2–3 garlic cloves, crushed
1–2 red chillies, seeded and
  finely chopped
400 g/14 oz can chopped tomatoes
45 ml/3 tbsp concentrated
  tomato purée
5 ml/1 tsp mixed dried herbs
450 ml/³/₄ pint l³/₄ cups water
450 g/1 lb pipe rigate
400 g/14 oz can red kidney
  beans, drained
salt and ground black pepper

garlic

onion

red chilli

red kidney beans

tomato purée

pipe rigate

chopped tomatoes

minced beef

1 Cook the minced beef or turkey in a non-stick saucepan, breaking up any large pieces with a wooden spoon until browned all over.

2 Add the onion, garlic and chilli, cover with a lid and cook gently for 5 minutes.

NUTRITIONAL NOTES

PER PORTION:

ENERGY 425Kcals/1785KJ **FAT** 5.4g
SATURATED FAT 1.4g **CHOLESTEROL** 44mg
CARBOHYDRATE 70g **FIBRE** 6.1g

3 Add the tomatoes, tomato purée, herbs, water and seasoning. Bring to the boil and simmer for 1¹/₂ hours. Leave to cool slightly.

4 Cook the pasta in a large pan of boiling, salted water until *al dente*. Drain thoroughly. Skim off any fat from the surface of the mince. Add the red kidney beans and heat for 5–10 minutes. Pour over the cooked pasta, and serve.

Turkey and Pasta Bake

Serves 4

INGREDIENTS
275 g/10 oz minced turkey
150 g/5 oz smoked turkey
    rashers, chopped
1–2 garlic cloves, crushed
1 onion, finely chopped
2 carrots, diced
30 ml/2 tbsp concentrated
    tomato purée
300 ml/½ pint/1¼ cups
    chicken stock
225 g/8 oz rigatoni
30 ml/2 tbsp grated
    Parmesan cheese
salt and ground black pepper

turkey rashers *carrots* *onion*

rigatoni

garlic

tomato purée

Parmesan cheese

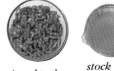

minced turkey *stock*

1 Brown the minced turkey in a non-stick saucepan, breaking up any large pieces with a wooden spoon, until well browned all over.

2 Add the chopped turkey rashers, garlic, onion, carrots, purée, stock and seasoning. Bring to the boil, cover and simmer for 1 hour until tender.

3 Preheat the oven to 180°C/350°F/Gas 4. Cook the pasta in a large pan of boiling, salted water until *al dente*. Drain thoroughly and mix with the turkey sauce.

4 Transfer to a shallow ovenproof dish and sprinkle with grated Parmesan cheese. Bake in the preheated oven for 20–30 minutes until lightly browned.

NUTRITIONAL NOTES

PER PORTION:

ENERGY 391Kcals/1641KJ **FAT** 4.9g
SATURATED FAT 2.2g **CHOLESTEROL** 60mg
CARBOHYDRATE 55g **FIBRE** 3.5g

Ham-filled Paprika Ravioli

Serves 4

INGREDIENTS
225 g/8 oz cooked smoked ham
60 ml/4 tbsp mango chutney
1 quantity of basic pasta dough,
    with 5 ml/1 tsp ground
    paprika added
egg white, beaten
flour, for dusting
1–2 garlic cloves, crushed
1 stick celery, sliced
50 g/2 oz sun-dried tomatoes
1 red chilli, seeded and chopped
150 ml/¼ pint/⅔ cup red wine
400 g/14 oz can chopped tomatoes
5 ml/1 tsp chopped fresh thyme,
    plus extra to garnish
10 ml/2 tsp caster sugar
salt and ground black pepper

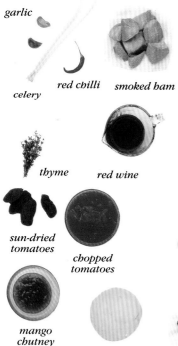

garlic

celery   *red chilli*   *smoked ham*

thyme   *red wine*

sun-dried tomatoes   *chopped tomatoes*

mango chutney   *basic pasta dough*   *paprika*

1 Remove all traces of fat from the ham, place it with the mango chutney in a food processor or blender and mince the mixture finely.

2 Roll the pasta into thin sheets and lay one piece over a ravioli tray. Put a teaspoonful of the ham filling into each of the depressions.

3 Brush around the edges of each ravioli with egg white. Cover with another sheet of pasta and press the edges well together to seal.

4 Using a rolling-pin, roll over the top of the dough to cut and seal each pocket. Transfer to a floured dish towel and rest for 1 hour before cooking.

5 Put the garlic, celery, sun-dried tomatoes, chilli, wine, canned tomatoes and thyme into a pan. Cover and cook for 15–20 minutes. Season with salt, pepper and sugar.

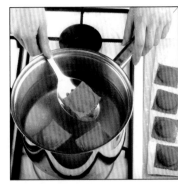

6 Cook the ravioli in a large pan of boiling, salted water for 4–5 minutes. Drain thoroughly. Spoon a little of the sauce on to a serving plate and arrange the ravioli on top. Sprinkle with fresh thyme and serve at once.

NUTRITIONAL NOTES
PER PORTION:

ENERGY 380Kcals/1594KJ **FAT** 7.6g
SATURATED FAT 2.1g **CHOLESTEROL** 152mg
CARBOHYDRATE 52g **FIBRE** 2.4g

Devilled Ham and Pineapple Salad

Serves 4

INGREDIENTS
225 g/8 oz wholewheat penne
150 ml/¼ pint/⅔ cup low-fat yogurt
15 ml/1 tbsp cider vinegar
5 ml/1 tsp wholegrain mustard
large pinch of caster sugar
30 ml/2 tbsp hot mango chutney
115 g/4 oz cooked lean ham, cubed
200 g/7 oz can pineapple chunks
2 sticks celery, chopped
½ green pepper, seeded and diced
15 ml/1 tbsp flaked toasted
    almonds, chopped roughly
salt and ground black pepper
crusty bread, to serve

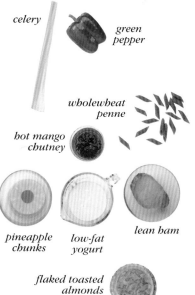

celery

green pepper

wholewheat penne

hot mango chutney

pineapple chunks

low-fat yogurt

lean ham

flaked toasted almonds

I Cook the pasta in a large pan of boiling, salted water until *al dente*. Drain and rinse thoroughly. Leave to cool.

2 To make the dressing, mix the yogurt, vinegar, mustard, sugar and mango chutney together. Season, add the pasta and toss lightly together.

3 Transfer the pasta to a serving dish. Scatter over the ham, pineapple, celery and pepper.

4 Sprinkle the top with toasted almonds. Serve with crusty bread.

NUTRITIONAL NOTES

PER PORTION:

ENERGY 303Kcals/1273KJ **FAT** 5.4g
SATURATED FAT 0.9g **CHOLESTEROL** 18.5mg
CARBOHYDRATE 51g **FIBRE** 6g

Curried Chicken Salad

Serves 4

INGREDIENTS

2 cooked chicken breasts, boned
175 g/6 oz French beans
350 g/12 oz multi-coloured penne
150 ml/¼ pint/⅔ cup low-fat yogurt
5 ml/1 tsp mild curry powder
1 garlic clove, crushed
1 green chilli, seeded and
    finely chopped
30 ml/2 tbsp chopped
    fresh coriander
4 firm ripe tomatoes, skinned,
    seeded and cut in strips
salt and ground black pepper
coriander leaves, to garnish

*multi-coloured
penne*

*chicken
breasts*

*green
chilli*

coriander

French beans

low-fat yogurt

tomatoes

garlic

1 Remove the skin from the chicken and cut in strips. Cut the green beans in 2.5 cm/1 in lengths and cook in boiling water for 5 minutes. Drain and rinse under cold water.

2 Cook the pasta in a large pan of boiling, salted water until *al dente*. Drain and rinse thoroughly.

3 To make the sauce, mix the yogurt, curry powder, garlic, chilli and chopped coriander together in a bowl. Stir in the chicken pieces and leave to stand for 30 minutes.

4 Transfer the pasta to a glass bowl and toss with the beans and tomatoes. Spoon over the chicken and sauce. Garnish with coriander leaves.

NUTRITIONAL NOTES

PER PORTION:

ENERGY 449Kcals/1884KJ **FAT** 5.1g
SATURATED FAT 1.3g **CHOLESTEROL** 38mg
CARBOHYDRATE 74g **FIBRE** 4.9g

Duck Breast Salad

Serves 6

INGREDIENTS

2 duck breasts, boned
5 ml/1 tsp coriander seeds, crushed
350 g/12 oz rigatoni
150 ml/¼ pint/⅔ cup fresh
    orange juice
15 ml/1 tbsp lemon juice
10 ml/2 tsp runny honey
1 shallot, finely chopped
1 garlic clove, crushed
1 stick celery, chopped
75 g/3 oz dried cherries
45 ml/3 tbsp port
15 ml/1 tbsp chopped fresh mint,
    plus extra for garnish
30 ml/2 tbsp chopped fresh
    coriander, plus extra for garnish
1 eating apple, diced
2 oranges, segmented
salt and ground black pepper

coriander

rigatoni *port* *coriander seeds*

duck breasts

orange

mint

apple

shallot *dried cherries*

garlic

celery

1 Remove the skin and fat from the duck breasts and season with salt and pepper. Rub with crushed coriander seeds. Preheat the grill, then grill for 7–10 minutes depending on size. Wrap in foil and leave for 20 minutes.

2 Cook the pasta in a large pan of boiling, salted water until *al dente*. Drain thoroughly and rinse under cold running water. Leave to cool.

3 To make the dressing, put the orange juice, lemon juice, honey, shallot, garlic, celery, cherries, port, mint and fresh coriander into a bowl, whisk together and leave to marinate for 30 minutes.

4 Slice the duck very thinly. (It should be pink in the centre.)

5 Put the pasta into a bowl, add the dressing, diced apple and segments of orange. Toss well to coat the pasta. Transfer the salad to a serving plate with the duck slices and garnish with the extra coriander and mint.

NUTRITIONAL NOTES
PER PORTION:

ENERGY 348Kcals/1460KJ **FAT** 3.8g
SATURATED FAT 0.9g **CHOLESTEROL** 55mg
CARBOHYDRATE 64g **FIBRE** 1.3g

Herbed Beef Salad

Serves 6

INGREDIENTS

450 g/1 lb beef fillet
450 g/1 lb fresh tagliatelle with sun-
dried tomatoes and herbs
115 g/4 oz cherry tomatoes
½ cucumber

MARINADE

15 ml/1 tbsp soy sauce
15 ml/1 tbsp sherry
5 ml/1 tsp root ginger, grated
1 garlic clove, crushed

HERB DRESSING

30–45 ml/2–3 tbsp horseradish
    sauce
150 ml/¼ pint/⅔ cup low-fat yogurt
1 garlic clove, crushed
30–45 ml/2–3 tbsp chopped fresh
    herbs (chives, parsley, thyme)
salt and ground black pepper

cherry
tomatoes

cucumber

fillet beef

root ginger

garlic

tagliatelle

thyme

low-fat
yogurt

horseradish
sauce

parsley

soy sauce

chives

1 Mix all the marinade ingredients together in a shallow dish, put the beef in and turn it over to coat it. Cover with clear film and leave for 30 minutes to allow the flavours to penetrate the meat.

2 Preheat the grill. Lift the fillet out of the marinade and pat it dry with kitchen paper. Place on a grill rack and grill for 8 minutes on each side, basting with the marinade during cooking.

3 Transfer to a plate, cover with foil and leave to stand for 20 minutes.

4 Put all the dressing ingredients into a bowl and mix thoroughly together. Cook the pasta according to the directions on the packet, drain thoroughly, rinse under cold water and leave to dry.

5 Cut the cherry tomatoes in half. Cut the cucumber in half lengthways, scoop out the seeds with a teaspoon and slice thinly into crescents.

6 Put the pasta, cherry tomatoes, cucumber and dressing into a bowl and toss to coat. Slice the beef thinly and arrange on a plate with the pasta salad.

NUTRITIONAL NOTES

PER PORTION:

ENERGY 374Kcals/1572KJ **FAT** 5.7g
SATURATED FAT 1.7g **CHOLESTEROL** 46mg
CARBOHYDRATE 57g **FIBRE** 2.9g

VEGETARIAN PASTA DISHES

Pasta Primavera

Serves 4

INGREDIENTS

225 g/8 oz thin asparagus spears,
  cut in half
115 g/4 oz mange-tout, topped
  and tailed
115 g/4 oz whole baby corn-on-
  the-cob
225 g/8 oz whole baby
  carrots, trimmed
1 small red pepper, seeded
  and chopped
8 spring onions, sliced
225 g/8 oz torchietti
150 ml/¼ pint/⅔ cup low-fat
  cottage cheese
150 ml/¼ pint/⅔ cup low-fat yogurt
15 ml/1 tbsp lemon juice
15 ml/1 tbsp chopped parsley
15 ml/1 tbsp snipped chives
skimmed milk (optional)
salt and ground black pepper
sun-dried tomato bread, to serve

red
pepper

parsley

baby corn-
on-the-cob

spring
onions

baby
carrots

lemon

chives

torchietti

mange-tout

asparagus
spears

low-fat
yogurt

low-fat
cottage cheese

1 Cook the asparagus spears in a pan of boiling, salted water for 3–4 minutes. Add the mange-tout halfway through the cooking time. Drain and rinse both under cold water.

2 Cook the baby corn, carrots, red pepper and spring onions in the same way until tender. Drain and rinse.

3 Cook the pasta in a large pan of boiling, salted water until *al dente*. Drain thoroughly.

NUTRITIONAL NOTES

PER PORTION:

ENERGY 320Kcals/1344KJ **FAT** 3.1g
SATURATED FAT 0.4g **CHOLESTEROL** 3mg
CARBOHYDRATE 58g **FIBRE** 6.2g

4 Put the cottage cheese, yogurt, lemon juice, parsley, chives and seasoning into a food processor or blender and process until smooth. Thin the sauce with skimmed milk, if necessary. Put into a large pan with the pasta and vegetables, heat gently and toss carefully. Transfer to a serving plate and serve with sun-dried tomato bread.

Tagliatelle with Mushrooms

Serves 4

INGREDIENTS

1 small onion, finely chopped
2 garlic cloves, crushed
150 ml/¼ pint/⅔ cup
   vegetable stock
225 g/8 oz mixed fresh mushrooms,
   such as field, chestnut, oyster,
   or chanterelles
60 ml/4 tbsp white or red wine
10 ml/2 tsp concentrated
   tomato purée
15 ml/1 tbsp soy sauce
5 ml/1 tsp chopped fresh thyme
30 ml/2 tbsp chopped fresh parsley
225 g/8 oz fresh sun-dried tomato
   and herb tagliatelle
salt and ground black pepper
shavings of Parmesan cheese,
   to serve (optional)

tomato purée   Parmesan cheese   onion

mixed mushrooms

thyme   parsley   vegetable stock

garlic

white wine   tagliatelle

soy sauce

1 Put the onion and garlic into a pan with the stock. Then cover and cook for 5 minutes or until tender.

2 Add the mushrooms (quartered or sliced if large or left whole if small), wine, purée and soy sauce. Cover and cook for 5 minutes.

NUTRITIONAL NOTES
PER PORTION:

ENERGY 241Kcals/1010KJ **FAT** 2.4g
SATURATED FAT 0.7g **CHOLESTEROL** 3mg
CARBOHYDRATE 45g **FIBRE** 3g

3 Remove the lid from the pan and boil until the liquid has reduced by half. Stir in the chopped fresh herbs and season to taste.

4 Cook the pasta in a large pan of boiling, salted water until *al dente*. Drain thoroughly and toss lightly with the mushrooms. Serve at once with shavings of Parmesan cheese, if using.

Vegetarian Lasagne

Serves 6–8

INGREDIENTS
1 small aubergine
1 large onion, finely chopped
2 garlic cloves, crushed
150 ml/¼ pint/⅔ cup
   vegetable stock
225 g/8 oz mushrooms, sliced
400 g/14 oz can chopped tomatoes
30 ml/2 tbsp tomato purée
150 ml/¼ pint/⅔ cup red wine
1.5 ml/¼ tsp ground ginger
5 ml/1 tsp mixed dried herbs
10–12 sheets lasagne
salt and pepper
25 g/1 oz low-fat margarine
25 g/1 oz plain flour
300 ml/½ pint/1¼ cups
   skimmed milk
large pinch of grated nutmeg
200 g/7 oz low-fat cottage cheese
1 egg, beaten
15 g/½ oz grated Parmesan cheese
25 g/1 oz reduced-fat Cheddar
   cheese, grated
salt and ground black pepper

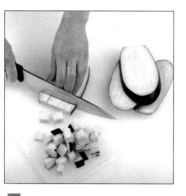

1 Wash the aubergine and cut it into 2.5 cm/1 in cubes. Put the onion and garlic into a saucepan with the stock, cover and cook for about 5 minutes or until tender.

2 Add the diced aubergine, sliced mushrooms, tomatoes, tomato purée, wine, ginger, seasoning and herbs. Bring to the boil, cover and cook for 15–20 minutes. Remove the lid and cook rapidly to evaporate the liquid by half.

3 To make the sauce, put the margarine, flour, skimmed milk and nutmeg into a pan. Whisk together over the heat until thickened and smooth. Season to taste.

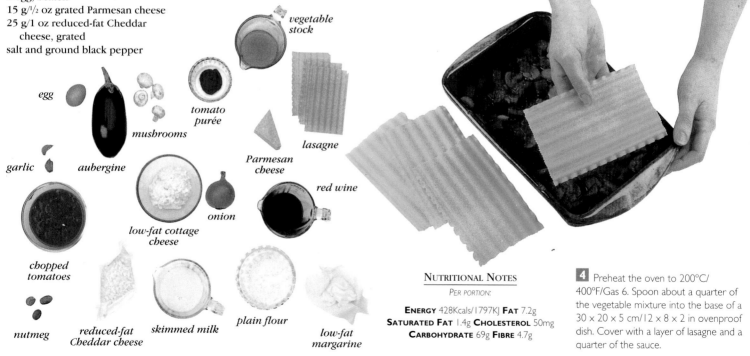

egg

vegetable stock

mushrooms

tomato purée

lasagne

garlic *aubergine*

Parmesan cheese

red wine

onion

low-fat cottage cheese

chopped tomatoes

nutmeg *reduced-fat Cheddar cheese* *skimmed milk* *plain flour* *low-fat margarine*

NUTRITIONAL NOTES
PER PORTION:

ENERGY 428Kcals/1797KJ **FAT** 7.2g
SATURATED FAT 1.4g **CHOLESTEROL** 50mg
CARBOHYDRATE 69g **FIBRE** 4.7g

4 Preheat the oven to 200°C/400°F/Gas 6. Spoon about a quarter of the vegetable mixture into the base of a 30 × 20 × 5 cm/12 × 8 × 2 in ovenproof dish. Cover with a layer of lasagne and a quarter of the sauce.

5 Repeat with two more layers, then cover with the cottage cheese. Beat the egg into the remaining sauce and pour over the top. Sprinkle with the two grated cheeses.

6 Bake for 25–30 minutes or until the top is golden brown.

Crescent Spinach Ravioli

Serves 4–6

INGREDIENTS

bunch of spring onions,
    finely chopped
1 carrot, coarsely grated
2 garlic cloves, crushed
200 g/7 oz low-fat cottage cheese
15 ml/1 tbsp chopped dill
4 halves sun-dried tomatoes,
    finely chopped
25 g/1 oz grated Parmesan cheese
1 quantity of basic pasta dough,
    with 115 g/4 oz frozen chopped
    spinach added
egg white, beaten, for brushing
flour, for dusting
salt and ground black pepper
2 halves sun-dried tomatoes, finely
    chopped, and fresh dill,
    to garnish

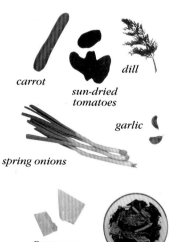

carrot

dill

sun-dried
tomatoes

garlic

spring onions

Parmesan
cheese

spinach

low-fat
cottage cheese

1 Put the spring onions, carrot, garlic and cottage cheese into a bowl. Add the chopped dill, tomatoes, seasoning and Parmesan cheese.

2 Roll the spinach pasta into thin sheets, cut into 7.5 cm/3 in rounds with a fluted pastry cutter.

3 Place a dessertspoon of filling in the centre of each circle. Brush the edges with egg white.

4 Fold each in half to make crescents. Press the edges together to seal. Transfer to a floured dish towel to rest for 1 hour before cooking. Makes about 80 crescents.

5 Cook the pasta in a large pan of boiling, salted water for 5 minutes (cook in batches to stop them sticking together). Drain well.

6 Put the crescents on to warmed serving plates and garnish with sun-dried tomatoes and dill.

NUTRITIONAL NOTES
PER PORTION:

ENERGY 312Kcals/1309KJ **FAT** 7.3g
SATURATED FAT 2.4g **CHOLESTEROL** 119mg
CARBOHYDRATE 43g **FIBRE** 3.4g

Vegetarian Cannelloni

Serves 4–6

INGREDIENTS

1 onion, finely chopped
2 garlic cloves, crushed
2 carrots, coarsely grated
2 sticks celery, finely chopped
150 g/¼ pint/⅔ cup vegetable stock
115 g/4 oz red or green lentils
400 g/14 oz can chopped tomatoes
30 ml/2 tbsp tomato purée
2.5 ml/½ tsp ground ginger
5 ml/1 tsp fresh thyme
5 ml/1 tsp chopped fresh rosemary
40 g/1½ oz low-fat margarine
40 g/1½ oz plain flour
600 ml/1 pint/2½ cups
    skimmed milk
1 bay leaf
large pinch grated nutmeg
16–18 cannelloni
25 g/1 oz reduced-fat Cheddar
    cheese, grated
25 g/1 oz grated Parmesan cheese
25 g/1 oz fresh white breadcrumbs
salt and ground black pepper
flat leaf parsley, to garnish

plain flour

low-fat margarine

reduced-fat Cheddar cheese

onion *garlic* *celery* *rosemary*

white breadcrumbs

bay leaf *thyme*

red lentils *Parmesan cheese* *skimmed milk*

carrots

nutmeg

chopped tomatoes *vegetable stock* *tomato purée*

cannelloni tubes

1 To make the filling put the onion, garlic, carrots and celery into a large saucepan, add half the stock, cover and cook for 5 minutes or until tender.

2 Add the lentils, chopped tomatoes, tomato purée, ginger, thyme, rosemary and seasoning. Bring to the boil, cover and cook for 20 minutes. Remove the lid and cook for about 10 minutes until thick and soft. Leave to cool.

3 To make the sauce, put the margarine, flour; skimmed milk and bay leaf into a pan and whisk over the heat until thick and smooth. Season with salt, pepper and nutmeg. Discard the bay leaf.

4 Fill the uncooked cannelloni by piping the filling into each tube. (It is easiest to hold them upright with one end flat on a board, while piping into the other end.)

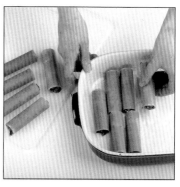

5 Preheat the oven to 180°C/350°F/ Gas 4. Spoon half the sauce into the bottom of a 20 cm/8 in square ovenproof dish. Lay two rows of filled cannelloni on top and spoon over the remaining sauce.

6 Scatter over the cheeses and breadcrumbs. Bake in the preheated oven for 30–40 minutes. Grill to brown the top, if necessary. Garnish with flat leaf parsley.

NUTRITIONAL NOTES
PER PORTION:

ENERGY 579Kcals/2432KJ FAT 9.8g
SATURATED FAT 2.7g CHOLESTEROL 13mg
CARBOHYDRATE 100g FIBRE 5.7g

Tagliatelle with Spinach Gnocchi

Serves 4–6

INGREDIENTS
450 g/1 lb mixed flavoured
    tagliatelle
flour, for dusting
shavings of Parmesan cheese,
    to garnish

SPINACH GNOCCHI
450 g/1 lb frozen chopped spinach
1 small onion, finely chopped
1 garlic clove, crushed
1.5 ml/¼ tsp ground nutmeg
400 g/14 oz low-fat cottage cheese
115 g/4 oz dried white breadcrumbs
75 g/3 oz semolina or plain flour
50 g/2 oz grated Parmesan cheese
3 egg whites
salt and pepper

TOMATO SAUCE
1 onion, finely chopped
1 stick celery, finely chopped
1 red pepper, seeded and diced
1 garlic clove, crushed
150 ml/¼ pint/⅔ cup
    vegetable stock
400 g/14 oz can tomatoes
15 ml/1 tbsp tomato purée
10 ml/2 tsp caster sugar
5 ml/1 tsp dried oregano

1 To make the tomato sauce, put the chopped onion, celery, pepper and garlic into a non-stick pan. Add the stock, bring to the boil and cook for 5 minutes or until tender.

2 Add the tomatoes, tomato purée, sugar and oregano. Season to taste, bring to the boil and simmer for 30 minutes until thick, stirring occasionally.

3 Meanwhile, put the frozen spinach, onion and garlic into a saucepan, cover and cook until the spinach is defrosted. Remove the lid and increase the heat to drive off any moisture. Season with salt, pepper and nutmeg. Cool the spinach in a bowl, add the remaining ingredients and mix thoroughly.

celery

garlic

egg

nutmeg

onion

low-fat cottage cheese

flavoured tagliatelle

red pepper

grated Parmesan cheese

spinach

dried white breadcrumbs

vegetable stock

tomato purée

tomatoes

semolina

4 Shape the mixture into about 24 ovals with two dessertspoons and place them on a lightly floured tray. Place in the fridge for 30 minutes.

78

5 Have a large shallow pan of boiling, salted water ready. Cook the gnocchi in batches, for about 5 minutes (the water should simmer gently and not boil). As soon as the gnocchi rise to the surface, remove them with a slotted spoon and drain thoroughly.

6 Cook the tagliatelle in a large pan of boiling, salted water until *al dente*. Drain thoroughly. Transfer to warmed serving plates, top with gnocchi and spoon over the tomato sauce. Scatter with shavings of Parmesan cheese and serve at once.

NUTRITIONAL NOTES
PER PORTION:

ENERGY 789Kcals/3315KJ **FAT** 10.9g
SATURATED FAT 3.7g **CHOLESTEROL** 20mg
CARBOHYDRATE 135g **FIBRE** 8.1g

Tofu Stir-fry with Egg Noodles

Serves 4

INGREDIENTS

225 g/8 oz firm smoked tofu
45 ml/3 tbsp dark soy sauce
30 ml/2 tbsp sherry or vermouth
3 leeks, sliced thinly
2.5 cm/1 in piece root ginger, peeled and finely grated
1–2 red chillies, seeded and sliced in rings
1 small red pepper, seeded and sliced thinly
150 ml/¼ pint/⅔ cup vegetable stock
10 ml/2 tsp runny honey
10 ml/2 tsp cornflour
225 g/8 oz medium egg noodles
salt and ground black pepper

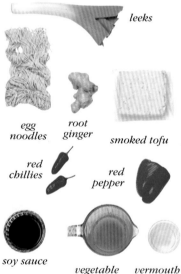

leeks

egg noodles *root ginger* *smoked tofu*

red chillies *red pepper*

soy sauce *vegetable stock* *vermouth*

1 Cut the tofu into 2 cm/¾ in cubes. Put it into a bowl with the soy sauce and sherry or vermouth. Toss to coat each piece and leave to marinate for about 30 minutes.

2 Put the leeks, ginger, chilli, pepper and stock into a frying pan. Bring to the boil and cook quickly for 2–3 minutes until just soft.

3 Strain the tofu, reserving the marinade. Mix the honey and cornflour into the marinade.

4 Put the egg noodles into a large pan of boiling water and leave to stand for about 6 minutes until cooked (or follow the instructions on the packet).

5 Heat a non-stick frying pan and quickly fry the tofu until lightly golden brown on all sides.

6 In a saucepan, add the vegetable mixture to the tofu with the marinade, and stir well until the liquid is thick and glossy. Spoon on to the egg noodles and serve at once.

NUTRITIONAL NOTES

PER PORTION

ENERGY 345Kcals/1448KJ **FAT** 8.2g
SATURATED FAT 0.7g **CHOLESTEROL** 0mg
CARBOHYDRATE 55g **FIBRE** 2.5g

Ratatouille Penne Bake

Serves 6

INGREDIENTS

1 small aubergine
2 courgettes, thickly sliced
200 g/7 oz firm tofu, cubed
45 ml/3 tbsp dark soy sauce
1 garlic clove, crushed
10 ml/2 tsp sesame seeds
1 small red pepper, seeded
   and sliced
1 onion, finely chopped
1–2 garlic cloves, crushed
150 ml/¼ pint/⅔ cup
   vegetable stock
3 firm ripe tomatoes, skinned,
   seeded and quartered
15 ml/1 tbsp chopped mixed herbs
225 g/8 oz penne
salt and ground black pepper
crusty bread, to serve

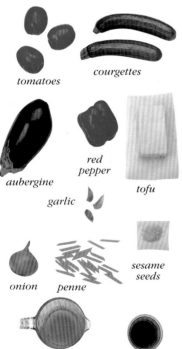

tomatoes   courgettes

aubergine   red pepper   tofu

garlic

sesame seeds

onion   penne

vegetable stock   soy sauce

1 Wash and cut the aubergine into 2.5 cm/1 in cubes. Put into a colander with the courgettes, sprinkle with salt and leave to drain for 30 minutes.

2 Mix the tofu with the soy sauce, garlic and sesame seeds. Cover and marinate for 30 minutes.

NUTRITIONAL NOTES
PER PORTION:

ENERGY 208Kcals/873KJ **FAT** 3.7g
SATURATED FAT 0.5g **CHOLESTEROL** 0mg
CARBOHYDRATE 36g **FIBRE** 3.9g

3 Put the pepper, onion and garlic into a saucepan, with the stock. Bring to the boil, cover and cook for 5 minutes until tender. Remove the lid and boil until all the stock has evaporated. Add the tomatoes and herbs and cook for a further 3 minutes. Season to taste.

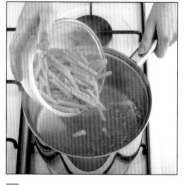

4 Meanwhile cook the pasta in a large pan of boiling, salted water until *al dente*. Drain thoroughly. Toss the pasta with the vegetables and tofu. Transfer to a shallow 25 cm/10 in square ovenproof dish and grill until lightly toasted. Transfer to a serving dish and serve with fresh crusty bread.

Chilli Mixed Bean Sauce

Serves 6

INGREDIENTS
1 onion, finely chopped
1–2 garlic cloves, crushed
1 large green chilli, seeded
   and chopped
150 ml/¼ pint/⅔ cup
   vegetable stock
400 g/14 oz can chopped tomatoes
30 ml/2 tbsp concentrated
   tomato purée
120 ml/4 fl oz/½ cup red wine
5 ml/1 tsp dried oregano
200 g/7 oz French beans, sliced
400 g/14 oz can red kidney
   beans, drained
400 g/14 oz can cannellini
   beans, drained
400 g/14 oz can chick-peas, drained
450 g/1 lb spaghetti
salt and ground black pepper

spaghetti

onion

green chilli

garlic

French beans

tomato purée

red kidney beans

cannellini beans

red wine

chopped tomatoes

vegetable stock

chick-peas

1 To make the sauce, put the chopped onion, garlic and chilli into a non-stick pan with the stock. Bring to the boil and cook for 5 minutes until tender.

2 Add the tomatoes, tomato purée, wine, seasoning and oregano. Bring to the boil, cover and simmer the sauce for 20 minutes.

NUTRITIONAL NOTES
PER PORTION:

ENERGY 431Kcals/1811KJ **FAT** 3.6g
SATURATED FAT 0.2g **CHOLESTEROL** 0mg
CARBOHYDRATE 82g **FIBRE** 9.9g

3 Cook the beans in boiling, salted water for about 5–6 minutes until tender. Drain thoroughly.

4 Add all the beans to the sauce and simmer for a further 10 minutes. Cook the spaghetti in a large pan of boiling, salted water until *al dente*. Drain thoroughly. Transfer to a serving dish and top with the chilli beans.

Spicy Chicken Salad

Serves 6

Ingredients

5 ml/1 tsp ground cumin seeds
5 ml/1 tsp ground paprika
5 ml/1 tsp ground turmeric
1–2 garlic cloves, crushed
30 ml/2 tbsp lime juice
4 chicken breasts, boned
    and skinned
225 g/8 oz rigatoni
1 red pepper, seeded and chopped
2 sticks celery, sliced thinly
1 shallot or small onion,
    finely chopped
25 g/1 oz stuffed green
    olives, halved
30 ml/2 tbsp runny honey
15 ml/1 tbsp wholegrain mustard
15–30 ml/1–2 tbsp lime juice
salt and ground black pepper
mixed salad leaves, to serve

honey

chicken breasts

cumin seeds

red pepper

onion

lime

turmeric *garlic*

celery

mixed salad leaves

rigatoni *stuffed olives* *paprika*

1 Mix the cumin, paprika, turmeric, garlic, seasoning and lime juice in a bowl. Rub this mixture over the chicken breasts. Lay in a shallow dish, cover with clear film and leave in a cool place for about 3 hours or overnight.

2 Preheat the oven to 200°C/400°F/ Gas 6. Put the chicken on a grill rack in a single layer and bake for 20 minutes. (Or grill for 8–10 minutes on each side.)

3 Cook the rigatoni in a large pan of boiling, salted water until *al dente*. Drain and rinse under cold water. Leave to drain thoroughly.

4 Put the red pepper, celery, shallot or small onion and olives into a large bowl with the pasta.

5 Mix the honey, mustard and lime juice together in a bowl and pour over the pasta. Toss to coat.

6 Cut the chicken in bite-size pieces. Arrange the mixed salad leaves on a serving dish, spoon the pasta mixture in the centre and top with the spicy chicken pieces.

Nutritional Notes
Per portion

Energy 277Kcals/1165KJ **Fat** 5.6g
Saturated Fat 1.4g **Cholesterol** 49mg
Carbohydrate 36g **Fibre** 2.1g

Piquant Chicken with Spaghetti

Serves 4

INGREDIENTS

1 onion, finely chopped
1 carrot, diced
1 garlic clove, crushed
300 ml/½ pint/1¼ cups vegetable
    stock or water
4 small chicken breasts, boned
    and skinned
bouquet garni (bay leaf, parsley
    stalks and thyme)
115 g/4 oz button mushrooms,
    sliced thinly
5 ml/1 tsp wine vinegar or
    lemon juice
350 g/12 oz spaghetti
½ cucumber, peeled and cut
    into fingers
2 firm ripe tomatoes, skinned,
    seeded and chopped
30 ml/2 tbsp low-fat crème fraîche
15 ml/1 tbsp chopped fresh parsley
15 ml/1 tbsp snipped chives
salt and ground black pepper

carrot

chicken breasts

tomatoes

cucumber

chives

spaghetti

thyme

parsley

button
mushrooms

vegetable stock

onion

bay leaf

1 Put the onion, carrot, garlic, stock or water into a saucepan with the chicken breasts and bouquet garni. Bring to the boil, cover and simmer gently for 15–20 minutes or until tender. Transfer the chicken to a plate and cover with foil.

2 Remove the chicken and strain the liquid. Discard the vegetables and return the liquid to the pan. Add the sliced mushrooms, wine vinegar or lemon juice and simmer for 2–3 minutes until tender.

3 Cook the spaghetti in a large pan of boiling, salted water until *al dente*. Drain thoroughly.

4 Blanch the cucumber in boiling water for 10 seconds. Drain and rinse under cold water.

5 Cut the chicken breasts into bite-size pieces. Boil the stock to reduce by half, then add the chicken, tomatoes, crème fraîche, cucumber and herbs. Season with salt and pepper to taste.

6 Transfer the spaghetti to a warmed serving dish and spoon over the piquant chicken. Serve at once.

NUTRITIONAL NOTES

PER PORTION:

ENERGY 472Kcals/1981KJ **FAT** 7.6g
SATURATED FAT 2.5g **CHOLESTEROL** 65mg
CARBOHYDRATE 72g **FIBRE** 4.8g

Pappardelle and Provençal Sauce

Serves 4

INGREDIENTS

2 small purple onions, peeled
150 ml/¼ pint/⅔ cup
    vegetable stock
1–2 garlic cloves, crushed
60 ml/4 tbsp red wine
2 courgettes, cut in fingers
1 yellow pepper, seeded and sliced
400 g/14 oz can tomatoes
10 ml/2 tsp fresh thyme
5 ml/1 tsp caster sugar
350 g/12 oz pappardelle
salt and ground black pepper
fresh thyme and 6 black olives,
    stoned and roughly chopped,
    to garnish

yellow pepper

purple onions

courgettes

thyme

pappardelle

black olives

tomatoes

garlic

vegetable stock

red wine

1 Cut each onion into eight wedges through the root end, to hold them together during cooking. Put into a saucepan with the stock and garlic. Bring to the boil, cover and simmer for 5 minutes until tender.

2 Add the red wine, courgettes, yellow pepper, tomatoes, thyme, sugar and seasoning. Bring to the boil and cook gently for 5–7 minutes, shaking the pan occasionally to coat the vegetables with the sauce. (Do not overcook the vegetables as they are much nicer if they are slightly crunchy.)

3 Cook the pasta in a large pan of boiling, salted water until *al dente*. Drain thoroughly.

4 Transfer the pasta to a warmed serving dish and top with the vegetables. Garnish with fresh thyme and chopped black olives.

NUTRITIONAL NOTES

PER PORTION:

ENERGY 369Kcals/1550KJ **FAT** 2.5g
SATURATED FAT 0.4g **CHOLESTEROL** 0mg
CARBOHYDRATE 75g **FIBRE** 4.3g

Fettuccine with Broccoli and Garlic

Serves 4

INGREDIENTS
3–4 garlic cloves, crushed
350 g/12 oz broccoli florets
150 ml/¼ pint/⅔ cup chicken stock
60 ml/4 tbsp white wine
30 ml/2 tbsp chopped fresh basil
60 ml/4 tbsp grated
   Parmesan cheese
350 g/12 oz fettuccine or tagliatelle
salt and pepper
fresh basil leaves, to garnish

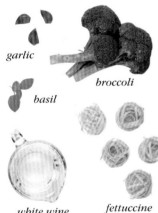

garlic

broccoli

basil

white wine *fettuccine*

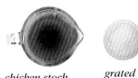

chicken stock   *grated Parmesan cheese*

1 Put the garlic, broccoli and stock into a saucepan. Bring to the boil and cook for 5 minutes until tender, stirring from time to time.

2 Mash with a fork or potato masher, until roughly chopped. Return to the pan with the white wine, basil and Parmesan cheese. Season to taste.

NUTRITIONAL NOTES
PER PORTION:

ENERGY 477Kcals/2002KJ **FAT** 8.3g
SATURATED FAT 3.4g **CHOLESTEROL** 15mg
CARBOHYDRATE 71g **FIBRE** 5g

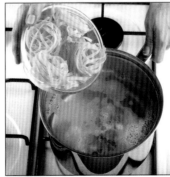

3 Cook the fettuccine in a large pan of boiling, salted water until *al dente*. Drain thoroughly.

4 Return to the pan with half the broccoli sauce, toss to coat the pasta and transfer to serving plates. Top with the remaining broccoli sauce and garnish with basil leaves.

Devilled Crab Conchiglioni

Serves 4

INGREDIENTS
350 g/12 oz conchiglioni (large
    pasta shells)
200 g/7 oz low-fat cream cheese
150 ml/¼ pint/⅔ cup skimmed milk
2.5 ml/½ tsp ground paprika
5 ml/1 tsp Dijon mustard
15 ml/1 tbsp dried breadcrumbs
10 ml/2 tsp grated Parmesan cheese
salt and pepper

FILLING
1 shallot, finely chopped
1 stick celery, finely chopped
½ small red pepper, seeded and
    finely chopped
45 ml/3 tbsp white wine
45 ml/3 tbsp low-fat crème fraîche
2 x 175 g/6 oz cans crab meat in
    brine, drained
45 ml/3 tbsp fresh white
    breadcrumbs
30 ml/2 tbsp grated
    Parmesan cheese
15 ml/1 tbsp Dijon mustard
2.5 ml/½ tsp red chilli paste

red pepper

*low-fat
cream cheese*

*grated
Parmesan
cheese*

*low-fat
crème
fraîche*

*dried
breadcrumbs*

crab meat

paprika

shallot   *celery*

conchiglioni   *white bread*

skimmed milk

white wine

1 Put the chopped shallot, celery and red pepper into a small pan with the white wine, cover and cook gently for 3–4 minutes until tender and the wine has evaporated.

2 Draw off the heat and add the crème fraîche, crab meat, fresh breadcrumbs, Parmesan, mustard, seasoning and chilli paste. Mix well.

3 Cook the pasta shells in a large pan of boiling, salted water until *al dente*. Drain well, then arrange upside-down on a clean dish towel to dry.

4 Put the cream cheese, milk, ground paprika and mustard into a small pan. Heat gently and whisk until smooth. Season to taste.

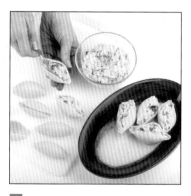

5 Preheat the oven to 220°C/425°F/ Gas 7. Fill the pasta shells with the crab mixture, spoon the cheese sauce over the base of a shallow ovenproof dish and arrange the shells on top.

6 Mix together the dried breadcrumbs and Parmesan cheese and sprinkle over the shells. Cover the dish with foil and bake for 15 minutes. Uncover and return to the oven for a further 5 minutes. Serve at once.

NUTRITIONAL NOTES
PER PORTION:

ENERGY 514Kcals/2159KJ **FAT** 8.8g
SATURATED FAT 3.5g **CHOLESTEROL** 79mg
CARBOHYDRATE 75g **FIBRE** 3.3g

Penne with Spinach

Serves 4

INGREDIENTS
225 g/8 oz fresh spinach
1 garlic clove, crushed
1 shallot or small onion,
    finely chopped
1/2 small red pepper, seeded and
    finely chopped
1 small red chilli, seeded
    and chopped
150 ml/1/4 pint/2/3 cup stock
350 g/12 oz penne
150 g/5 oz smoked turkey rashers
45 ml/3 tbsp low-fat crème fraîche
30 ml/2 tbsp grated
    Parmesan cheese
shavings of Parmesan cheese,
    to garnish

red pepper

grated Parmesan cheese

red chilli

shallot

smoked turkey rashers

penne

stock

low-fat crème fraîche

garlic

spinach

1 Wash the spinach and remove the hard central stalks. Shred finely.

2 Put the garlic, shallot or small onion, pepper and chilli into a large frying pan. Add the stock, cover and cook for about 5 minutes until tender. Add the prepared spinach and cook quickly for a further 2–3 minutes until it has wilted.

3 Cook the pasta in a large pan of boiling, salted water until *al dente*. Drain thoroughly.

4 Grill the smoked turkey rashers, cool a little, and chop finely.

5 Stir the crème fraîche and grated Parmesan into the pasta with the spinach, and toss carefully together.

6 Transfer to serving plates and sprinkle with chopped turkey and shavings of Parmesan cheese.

NUTRITIONAL NOTES

PER PORTION:

ENERGY 422Kcals/1772KJ **FAT** 6.8g
SATURATED FAT 3.2g **CHOLESTEROL** 38mg
CARBOHYDRATE 71g **FIBRE** 4.4g

Tagliatelle with Milanese Sauce

Serves 4

INGREDIENTS

1 onion, finely chopped
1 stick celery, finely chopped
1 red pepper, seeded and diced
1–2 garlic cloves, crushed
150 ml/¼ pint/⅔ cup
    vegetable stock
400 g/14 oz can tomatoes
15 ml/1 tbsp concentrated
    tomato purée
10 ml/2 tsp caster sugar
5 ml/1 tsp mixed dried herbs
350 g/12 oz tagliatelle
115 g/4 oz button
    mushrooms, sliced
60 ml/4 tbsp white wine
115 g/4 oz lean cooked ham, diced
salt and ground black pepper
15 ml/1 tbsp chopped fresh parsley,
    to garnish

garlic

celery

tagliatelle

red pepper

onion

lean cooked ham

button mushrooms

parsley

vegetable stock

tomatoes

white wine

tomato purée

1 Put the chopped onion, celery, pepper and garlic into a non-stick pan. Add the stock, bring to the boil and cook for 5 minutes or until tender.

2 Add the tomatoes, tomato purée, sugar and herbs. Season with salt and pepper. Bring to the boil, simmer for 30 minutes until thick. Stir occasionally.

3 Cook the pasta in a large pan of boiling, salted water until *al dente*. Drain thoroughly.

4 Put the mushrooms into a pan with the white wine, cover and cook for 3–4 minutes until tender and all the wine has been absorbed.

5 Add the mushrooms and diced ham to the tomato sauce. Reheat gently.

6 Transfer the pasta to a warmed serving dish and spoon on the sauce. Garnish with parsley.

NUTRITIONAL NOTES

Per portion:

ENERGY 405Kcals/1700KJ **FAT** 3.5g
SATURATED FAT 0.8g **CHOLESTEROL** 17mg
CARBOHYDRATE 77g **FIBRE** 4.5g

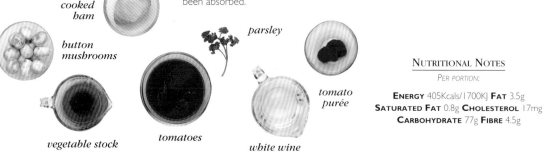

INDEX

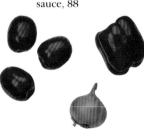

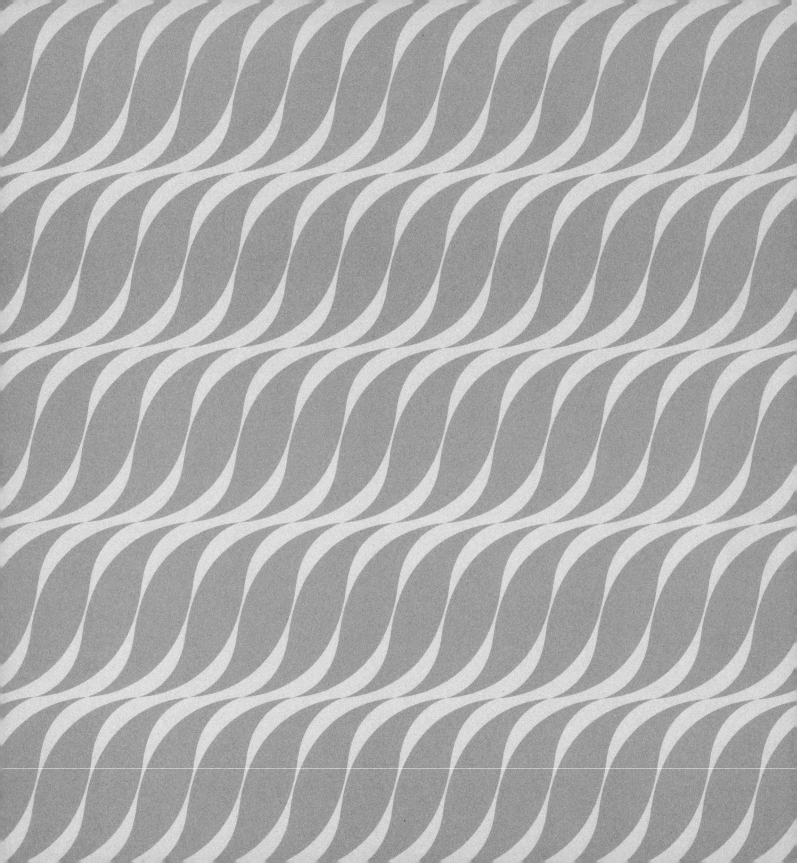